Naming and Framing

This book offers an innovative, unified theoretical model for better understanding the processes underpinning naming and framing and the power that words exert over human minds. The volume integrates theoretical paradigms and empirical insights from across a broad array of research disciplines, several of which have not been combined before, and uses this foundation as a point of departure for introducing its four-layered model of distinct but connected levels of analysis. Bringing insights from cognitive linguistics and psycholinguistics together with multimodal perspectives, Smith establishes new cross-disciplinary links, further integrating work from neighbouring fields such as marketing, health communication, and political communication, that indicate paths for future research and implications for communicative ethics and fairness.

This book will be of particular interest to students and scholars in multimodality, communication, semiotics, cognitive psychology, and linguistics, as well as those in related disciplines such as marketing, political communication, and health communication.

Viktor Smith has a PhD in International Business Communication and is an Associate Professor at the Department of Management, Society, and Communication, Copenhagen Business School. His key research interest is the way in which words in combination with other carriers of communicative content (pictures, colours, symbols, numbers, shapes, flavours, etc.) not only reflect, but shape the world around us, and the way we see it. Over the years, he has pursued and developed this interest both in cross-disciplinary theoretical work and relative to practice-oriented endeavours spanning from the convergence of European legal cultures to the development of best practices for fair consumer communication through product packaging design.

Routledge Studies in Multimodality
Edited by Kay L. O'Halloran, Curtin University

Shifts towards Image-centricity in Contemporary Multimodal Practices
Edited by Hartmut Stöckl, Helen Caple and Jana Pflaeging

Transmediations
Communication Across Media Borders
Edited by Niklas Salmose and Lars Elleström

Multimodal Approaches to Media Discourses
Reconstructing the Age of Austerity in the United Kingdom
Edited by Tim Griebel, Stefan Evert and Philipp Heinrich

Designing Learning with Embodied Teaching
Perspectives from Multimodality
Fei Victor Lim

Kinesemiotics
Modelling How Choreographed Movement Means in Space
Arianna Maiorani

Naming and Framing
Understanding the Power of Words across Disciplines, Domains, and Modalities
Viktor Smith

For more information about this series, please visit: https://www.routledge.com/Routledge-Studies-in-Multimodality/book-series/RSMM

Naming and Framing
Understanding the Power of Words across Disciplines, Domains, and Modalities

Viktor Smith

NEW YORK AND LONDON

First published 2021
by Routledge
52 Vanderbilt Avenue, New York, NY 10017

and by Routledge
2 Park Square, Milton Park, Abingdon, Oxon, OX14 4RN

Routledge is an imprint of the Taylor & Francis Group, an informa business

© 2021 Taylor & Francis

The right of Viktor Smith to be identified as author of this work has been asserted by him in accordance with sections 77 and 78 of the Copyright, Designs and Patents Act 1988.

All rights reserved. No part of this book may be reprinted or reproduced or utilised in any form or by any electronic, mechanical, or other means, now known or hereafter invented, including photocopying and recording, or in any information storage or retrieval system, without permission in writing from the publishers.

Trademark notice: Product or corporate names may be trademarks or registered trademarks, and are used only for identification and explanation without intent to infringe.

Library of Congress Cataloging-in-Publication Data
A catalog record for this title has been requested

ISBN: 978-0-367-50921-7 (hbk)
ISBN: 978-0-367-72593-8 (pbk)
ISBN: 978-1-003-05183-1 (ebk)

Typeset in Times New Roman by
codeMantra

Contents

Preface   vii
Acknowledgements   ix

Introduction   1
  0.1 What's in a Name – What's in a Frame? 1
  0.2 Aims and Scope 4
  0.3 Cross-Disciplinary Positioning 8

1 Naming & Framing at Level 1: Having a Name for It   11
  1.1 Naming Something Is Having It, but Who's to Decide? 11
  1.2 What Language(s) May and Must 13
  1.3 From ad-hoc Categories to First Candidates for Naming 18
    1.3.1 The Anatomy of Human Concepts 19
    1.3.2 A Dynamic Approach to Human Categorization 21
  1.4 Success Criteria for Naming at Level 1 Revisited 25

2 Naming & Framing at Level 2: The Joyce Principle   27
  2.1 Juliet's Wisdom versus Joyce's Creativity 27
  2.2 Limits to Lexical Arbitrariness: Names Talk! 28
  2.3 Additional Leads from Language Processing 33
  2.4 Lessons Learned from Joyce 37

3 Naming & Framing at Level 3: The Juliet Principle — 40
3.1 The Multimodal Character of Level 3 Framings 40
3.2 An Illustration: High- versus Low-Budget Route Framing of Brand and Product Names 43
   3.2.1 Consuming the "Semiotic Cocktail" 45
   3.2.2 Control versus Credibility and Effect 51
3.3 Names Negotiated 53
3.4 Is the Name Wrong or Is the World Going Wrong? 58

4 Naming & Framing at Level 4: The Lexical Toolbox of Issues Management and Its Multimodal Surroundings — 59
4.1 Beyond the Meaning of Individual Names 59
4.2 A Fractured Paradigm: Entman and Later Developments 60
4.3 Understanding the Full Ecosystem of Naming & Framing 62
4.4 Implications for Communicative Ethics and Fairness 65
4.5 Why Framing Works 67
   4.5.1 Stereotype Thinking 68
   4.5.2 Mental Shortcuts 69
   4.5.3 A Quest for Situational Relevance 69
4.6 Is Fair (Strategic) Communication Possible? 75

5 Concluding Remarks — 77

References 81
Index 105

Preface

My declared intention was to produce a concise book, at least for a first edition, and so I did. This may strike some readers as odd, given the title. Surely, the power that words exert over human minds must have been a cardinal concern for an immense number of thinkers and doers since the earliest days of humanity (let alone to artists, though that is in many ways a distinct domain which, alas, cannot be encompassed within the intended scope of this book). The subject is thus bound to have been approached from a multitude of theoretical and practical perspectives in support of a multitude of endeavours from saving marriages, establishing group identities, and substantiating legal claims to promoting commercial products and legitimizing wars. Could all of that really be encompassed in a single book, even a thicker one? Of course not, and that was not the intention.

But there is another side of that coin. The lasting and versatile attention to word power means that essential points, observations, and analyses with a strong potential for complementing each other remain scattered across a multitude of theoretical paradigms and day-to-day human concerns with few natural touchpoints. In other words, much of what could have been said to shed light on the subject as a whole has not yet been said, at least not in conjunction. Still, during the latest years, certain new cross-disciplinary links have been established with a potential for promoting further developments along these lines. This particularly applies to work presented under the heading of naming & framing (despite a so far rather blurring understanding of the phrasing itself) and under the agenda of multimodal communication research where words are seen as merely one (yet important) part of the total mix of verbal and nonverbal communicative resources that shape our world view.

My modest ambition with this book, then, is to take some aspects of these lines of reasoning a step further by suggesting that the power of words ultimately comes down to four different but connected enterprises: giving things names, deciding on what name to give them, further shaping people's understanding of these names through multimodal cotext, and selecting larger sets of names for presenting a given subject matter in a particular light. To further qualify this basic point, I draw on insights gained across a number of areas of research and practice, some of which have not traditionally been combined for the reasons just mentioned. At the same time, I have taken utmost care not to go any deeper into any specifics and technicalities of each of these fields than strictly required for maintaining the overall argument. The opposite would pose an obvious risk of losing (different) parts of the intended audience along the way. If the overall idea is well received, a second edition might, however, well leave room for extensions along several dimensions, ideally by encompassing new results gained in future collaborative cross-disciplinary work. However, at present, the major goal is to prepare the ground for such possible next steps.

Copenhagen, November 2020, Viktor Smith

Acknowledgements

I am much indebted to a number of colleagues and collaborators at Copenhagen Business School and far beyond (no one mentioned, no one forgotten) for valuable comments and ideas as the work progressed and for paving the ground for it in earlier discussions and in joint empirical work. Part of the latter was supported by the Danish Council for Strategic Research and by the Independent Research Fund Denmark. I owe special thanks to Per Durst-Andersen for getting me to wonder about the power of words in the first place, and for remaining a vital dialogue partner and friend ever since. On the publishing side, I am deeply indebted to Series Editor Kay O'Halloran, to Routledge Editor Elysse Preposi, and to two anonymous reviewers, for gently helping me find the right cut for the final book, and to Editorial Assistants Helena Parkinson and Mitchell Manners and to Project Manager Karthikeyan Subramaniam for keeping the publishing process on track. I am furthermore most grateful to Niklas Antonson and to Daniel Barratt for creating and/or modifying key illustrations (and to Daniel for an inspiring dialogue about other key issues as well). Likewise, I sincerely thank DHGate.com, Cavi-Art, and Michel Naglin, owner of boutique Home-Créa in Paris, for kindly allowing me to use their original visual material. As for Michel, I am equally (perhaps more) delighted with our inspiring discussions and exchanges of examples on the naming & framing of round objects (and other things) in French versus English as our email correspondence expanded. I am furthermore grateful to Pixabay.com and to Wikimedia Commons for facilitating unrestricted sharing of visual content. Great thanks also to my recent students in the BA course Multimodal Communication and the MSc course Marketing Campaigns at Copenhagen Business School for being a responsive and constructive test audience. Last but not least, I owe the hugest thanks to my family (parents, wife, kids, and our dog Sputnik), for bearing with me while I was immersed in the manuscript and neglected lots of more important things.

Introduction

0.1 What's in a Name – What's in a Frame?

The power that words have to not only refer to objects and phenomena in perceived reality but to make us aware of their presence and shape our understanding of them has been recognized and exploited by man since the earliest days of civilization (McWhorter, 2003; Thomas, 1992; Wood, 1991; Mey, 1985). Yet, the implications are possibly even more prominent in today's increasingly information- and communication-driven societies (Barton, 2016; Webster, 2014; Graham, 2004). What would *smartphones, fake news, hipsters, Brexit*, or *Covid-19* be to us if they had not become known as... precisely that? What makes some people prefer the name *sex worker* to *prostitute* when referring to the same individuals? What qualifies the word *apple* as a carrier of high expectations to IT devices? And why do we find it easier to support a *government* that is *defending* its *citizens* against *terrorists* (*separatists, coupists*) than a *regime* that is *oppressing* its *opposition* (*minorities, dissidents*), regardless that the words may well be applied to the same conflict by different interested parties? Understanding the mechanisms in play here seems to be worthwhile for academic, social, political, commercial, and ethical reasons.

However, the full array of mechanisms through which words exert their power over human minds has not as yet been subject to a unified theoretical analysis. Several directions of research take the study of words beyond pure linguistics (whether conceived in a structural, generative, functional, or other sense) and address the role that these entities (also) play in human cognition and social interaction. While a number of essential issues involving such perspectives have thus been investigated in substantial depth, the insights gained tend to remain isolated within disciplinary boundaries instead of being matched against each other to assess what each of them might contribute to a fuller understanding of the overall topic.

In the general linguistic, psychological, and philosophical literature, for example, much attention has been devoted to such essential sub-issues as the regularities underlying the formation and comprehension of new words (Müller, Ohnheiser, Olsen, & Rainer, 2015; Aitchison, 2012; Schmid, 2011; Benczes, 2006b; Goldberg, 2006; Libben & Jarema, 2006; Štekauer, 2005; Devitt & Sterelny, 1999: 66–113), and possible connections between the word stock of individual languages and the world views and styles of thinking of their speakers (Harley, 2014: 51–103; Kone, 2013; Deutscher, 2010; Gumperz & Levinson, 1996; Pinxten, 1976). However, the focus tends to remain on a generic level, i.e. on what can be observed for languages and their users viewed as monolithic entities. Less attention has been devoted to the unique micro-choices that individual language users (journalists, politicians, marketing executives, researchers, lawyers, bloggers, artists, and, ultimately, anybody) make when selecting and/or creating particular words to support a particular understanding of a given subject in preference to other conceivable ones; see May (1985: 7–18) for a related argument.

By contrast, such systematic uses of words and language to shape perceived reality have been dealt with in rhetoric since antiquity (Kennedy, 2008; Carey, 1994). More recently, the issue has furthermore gained substantial attention within and across several branches of the social sciences and humanities spanning from political science to functional linguistics (Mautner, 2016; Fairhurst, 2011; Vliegenthar & van Zoonen, 2011; Chong & Druckman, 2007; Fauconnier & Turner, 2003; Martin & White, 2003; Scheufele, 1999; Entman, 1993; Tannen, 1993; Goffman, 1974). Characteristically, these approaches tend to go beyond the individual word, focusing on how choosing between different sets of words, phrases, and non-verbal communicative means can be used for presenting a given subject in different ways, from arms control to climate change. In other words, the main attention tends to be devoted to what we shall label Level 4 of naming & framing analyses in the following, whereas Levels 1–3 are less systematically addressed.

Exceptions include the treatment of specific issues such as the persuasive use of conceptual blending and metaphor (Charteris-Black, 2011; Fauconnier & Lakoff, 2009; Fairhurst & Sarr, 1996) and the contribution of the choice of words to supporting positive or negative appraisals of the same situations and events (Martin & White, 2003; Scherer, Schorr, & Johnstone, 2001). Furthermore, the

Introduction 3

establishment of multimodal communication research as a distinct field of inquiry has contributed to shedding new light at the decisive role of nonverbal elements such as pictures, colours, shapes, and physical action in the framing (also) of individual words and vice versa (Powell, Boomgaarden, de Swert, & de Vreese, 2019; Meijers, Remmelswaal & Wonneberger, 2018; Jewitt, Bezemer, & O'Halloran, 2016; Jones, 2014).

The importance of choosing and/or creating "the right words" is also widely recognized in a variety of more performance-oriented disciplines. The list spans from journalism and media research (Lecheler, Bos, & Vliegenthart, 2015; D'Angelo & Kuypers, 2010; Matthes, 2009; McCombs, 1997), political communication (Schaffner & Sellers, 2010; Bizer & Petty, 2005; Apthorpe & Gasper, 1996), and public relations (Anderson, 2018, Luntz, 2007; Ledingham, 2003; Hallahan, 1999; Grunig & Hunt, 1984) to marketing and branding (Arora, Kalro, & Sharma, 2015; Riezebos, Kist, & Kootstra, 2003; Collins, 1977), business communications (Darics & Koller, 2017; Mautner, 2016), health promotion (Lynch & Zoller, 2015; Corcoran, 2013; Brown, 1995), legal argumentation (Rideout, 2008; Legrand, 1997a, b), and the management of professional terminologies (Kockaert & Steurs, 2015; Wright & Budin, 1997).[1] However, with some essential exceptions to be further addressed below, the emphasis tends to be either on the wider strategic reasons for exercising the power of words in the first place or on general persuasion and agenda-setting strategies suited for supporting such goals (O'Keefe, 2016; Corcoran, 2013; McCombs, 1997). The words that ultimately come to fulfil the strategic purposes, on the other hand, are often addressed in intuitive commonsense terms, relying on seemingly self-explanatory examples such as those given in the beginning of this section; see Mautner (2016: 1–6) for similar observations.

As we shall see shortly, however, the examples given earlier illustrate profoundly different reasons why and mechanisms through which words can exert a power over human minds, and these subtleties are not always clearly differentiated in the mainstream literature of the various fields just mentioned.

Still, attempts have been made to subsume the phenomena of interest, or some of them, under a common heading, in particular

---

1 The same applies to literature and the arts. However, this perspective entails additional considerations on artistic genres, conventions, and styles which would lead too far beyond the intended scope of the present book.

4 Introduction

that of *naming & framing*. This phrasing recurs in academic papers (Charette, Hooker, & Stanton, 2015; Herzog, 2007; Hoeyer, 2005; Brown, 1995), in practice-oriented recommendations (Mathews, 2016; Western States Center, 2003), and in the general debate (Park, 2014), yet with great variation in scope and theoretical positioning. Moreover, while the words *naming* and *framing* taken separately have several (even if diverse) established definitions, this is not the case with the present word combination which authors tend to treat as self-explanatory (as has been argued also for the specific communication-theoretical sense(s) of *framing*; see Entman, 1993: 52).

0.2 Aims and Scope

Against this background, the present book aims at taking the matter a step further by suggesting a hierarchy of four distinct yet tightly interwoven procedures and corresponding levels (or layers) of analysis that can be described as manifestations of naming & framing operations.

All of them have been addressed under these headings earlier, but rarely viewed in integration. Likewise, several other frameworks take a multi-layered approach to analysing words and their meanings in also addressing other levels of language structure (phonetics, syntax, text) and conceptual and contextual information presented by verbal and nonverbal means. Examples include, but are not exhausted by, the mapping of overarching functional patterns across linguistic forms in construction grammar (Goldberg, 2006; Fillmore, Kay, & O'Connor, 1988), theorizing on the interface between (code-based) semantics and (situational) pragmatics (Ariel, 2010; Zlatev, Smith, van de Weijer, & Skydsgaard, 2010; Verschueren, 1998) and between visual and verbal representations of composite communicative content (Forceville, 2014; Messaris, 1997), along with several frameworks supporting more practice-oriented enterprises from foreign language learning and teaching (Graves, August, & Mancilla-Martinez, 2013; Prince, 2006) to commercial product development and naming (Özcan & Egmond, 2012; Moskowitz, Reisner, Itty, Katz, & Krieger, 2006). What the present work might contribute to the general picture, then, is establishing a direct connection between some of the perspectives just mentioned, and others, and the quest set up initially: to yield a better understanding of the totality of mechanisms through which words exert their power over human minds.

In the existing literature, this perspective is most aptly captured by the intuitively appealing but so far vaguely defined notion of *naming & framing* as introduced in Section 0.1. We will continue the inquiry along that path, incorporating and expanding upon well-known core senses of the English words. The word *naming* will be used for referring to either creating a word for something (i.e. *giving it a name*) or selecting a well-known word among existing alternatives for referring to something (i.e. *calling it by a certain name*), a distinction that is not always made explicit in the existing literature. The word *framing*, in turn, will refer to the circumstance that something influences and delimits the understanding of something else in a particular direction. As we shall soon see, this is an apt description of more than one level of sense-making involving naming (see Table 0.1 and Figure 0.1) below.

Before proceeding, a few additional clarifications of terminology are required. The linguistic units that people use for naming things in either of the two senses mentioned will in their capacity as such also be referred to as *words*, apart from such instances where the more technical term *lexical expression(-unit)* has its justification. The latter is the case where it is essential to allow for the existence of orthographically and/or phonetically separate words that nevertheless function as "one word," i.e. as an indivisible whole the meaning of which goes beyond the meaning of its parts, e.g. *home banking*, *deep state*, *Bank of America*. Moreover, the term makes it possible to distinguish the sequence of sounds or letters as such from the meaning attached to it, whereas the word *word* is ambiguous in that respect; take the statements "the word *nerd* consists of 4 letters" versus "the word *nerd* sounds rather impolite." This is essential when the processes behind the very establishment of such a permanent link between expression and content are of primary interest. Finally, when words are referred to in their capacity as tools for *naming* something (in either of the two senses indicated), they are also labelled *names*. For the present purpose, the term covers both *proper names* (denoting individual objects such as *Donald Trump* or the *Eiffel Tower)* and *general names* (denoting categories of objects such as *Republican politician* or *tourist attraction*), notwithstanding that the word *name* is often reserved for the former purpose in everyday speech.

The distinctions made so far are all well-known and (relatively) uncontroversial, whereas the distinction between four levels of naming & framing is not and will be subject to further explanation and discussion in the following chapters. Table 0.1 gives a first overview of the four levels (or layers) of naming & framing suggested. The example *sleep hygiene* is repeated for all four levels to clarify the mutual connection between them. The same key points are rendered in visual form in Figure 0.1. To simplify things, the objects or phenomena to which the names in question are applied are referred to as "it."

It should be stressed from the outset that the four levels proposed do not *per se* pertain to different sorts of names but to different perspectives from which they can be viewed. What is said under Level 1 thus applies to any name by virtue of its very existence, while an agreement on its collectively adopted meaning ultimately depends on the factors mentioned under Level 3. If the expression-unit in question is not arbitrary to begin with, i.e. has a built-in sematic potential in its own right, the factors mentioned under Level 2 will function as a mediating link in the above-mentioned process with a potential for influencing its outcome in essential respects. Level 4, then, extends the perspective from single names (with all three perspectives potentially applicable to them) to larger sets of names selected to present a wider issue in a certain light in running communication. This, in turn, will feed contextual cues back to Level 3 with an impact also for the understanding of individual names, as potentially mediated by Level 2, and thereby affect the cognitive implications of the very existence of these names at Level 1.

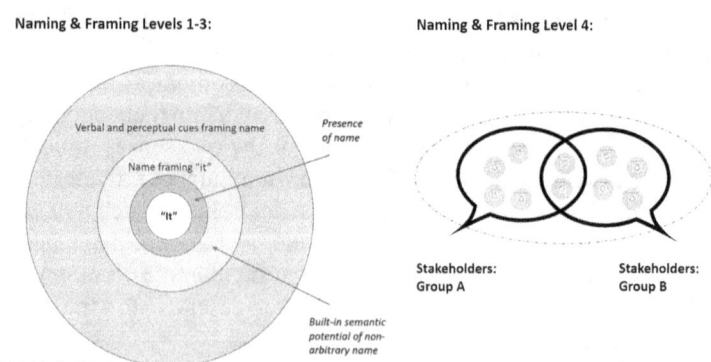

Figure 0.1 Four levels of naming & framing visualized.

Table 0.1 Four levels of naming & framing

Level 1	Framing of "it" as a potential object of human thinking and communication by virtue of the very fact of providing it with a dedicated name. ***Examples:*** *sleep hygiene, global warming, blogger, Brexit, nerd* (as opposed to no name).
Level 2	Additional framing of "it" emerging from the composition and/ or origin of the expression-unit chosen for the purpose which may emphasize some properties of "it" at the expense of others. ***Examples:*** *sleep hygiene* (presenting "it" as a kind of *hygiene*), *global warming* (which explains the nature of "it," but not why many people see it as a threat), *worm* (in the specific IT sense highlighting the similarities between a kind of computer malware and living worms), *sex worker* (which suggests a higher degree of societal legitimacy than *prostitute*), *Whopper* (which sounds like something big and mighty).
Level 3	Framing of the name itself by other words, sentences, and nonverbal perceptual cues surrounding it in running communication (including people's first-hand experiences with whatever it denotes) which further contribute to shaping its generally agreed meaning. ***Examples:*** the communicative processes and first-hand experiences that shaped the current understanding of *sleep hygiene* as a distinct medical field, of *global warming* as a major environmental concern, and of *Apple* as a carrier of high expectations to IT devices.
Level 4	Framing of a wider subject matter (constituting "it" in a wider, thematic sense) by referring to key aspects of it by means of different (in themselves often well-known) names and whole sets of names. ***Examples:*** the contribution of the names *sleep hygiene, sleep cycle, bedtime routines, powernap*, etc. to a particular understanding of the wider subject of sleeping problems and how to deal with them; the contribution of the names *global warming, greenhouse effect, CO_2 footprint, climate refugees*, etc., to global concerns about the wider subject of climate change; the different implications of the statements "the rebels fought courageously against the authoritarian regime" and "the government troops were ambushed by radicalized terrorists" (as applied to the same events by different stakeholders).

Note
  Levels 1–3 all relate to naming in the sense of 'giving something a name.' However, while the question at Level 1 is *whether* something has been given a name, the question at Level 2 is *how* it has been named, and the question at Level 3 is *how surrounding contextual cues* shape the full communicative potential of the name. By contrast, Level 4 relates to naming in the sense of 'calling something by a certain name' (or whole sets of names), thereby affecting people's understanding of whatever is talked about without necessarily creating new names for that purpose. In turn, all four procedures may be described as instances of framing in the sense of 'influencing and delimiting the understanding of something else.' The essential difference lies in what is framed by what at the respective levels, a differentiation which is often lacking in the existing naming & framing literature.

In the following, the framework and its applicability to real-life naming & framing processes will be taken further and matched against existing theoretical paradigms and empirical findings contributing different pieces to the overall puzzle.

0.3 Cross-Disciplinary Positioning

The approach is cross-disciplinary by the very nature of the matter, as it follows from the literature review given earlier. As such, it continues the agenda proposed by Entman (1993) in his much-quoted seminal study of (what we here call) naming & framing at Level 4, namely "bringing together insights and theories that would otherwise remain scattered in other disciplines" (1993: 51). Completing the analysis with a more detailed treatment of Levels 1–3, in turn, presupposes that "language is not treated in isolation (e.g. as a 'module'), but both as based on structures and processes of general cognition and social cognition and as affecting such structures and processes" (Scandinavian Association for Language and Cognition, cf. SALC, 2019). This further entails a dynamic interpretation of the classic Saussurean distinction between "langue" and "parole" (Saussure, 2011 [1916]), i.e. between human language(s) understood as an intersubjectively agreed code and individual people's concrete communicative interaction based on that code. What should never be left out of sight is that the code itself, including a shared vocabulary, is generated and continuously adjusted through the communicative efforts of concrete individuals in concrete situations pursuing concrete communicative goals, and that they may sometimes change or add new elements to the code in that process.

The latter insight has been articulated from a variety of paradigm-specific perspectives in language philosophy (taking both mentalist and radical realist shapes, e.g. Armstrong, 2016; Devitt & Sterelny, 1999: 66–113; Mulligan, 1990; Leopold, 1929), language psychology (Harley, 2014: 51–103; Cohen, 1986; Hörmann, 1986; 1981), cognitive pragmatics (Ariel, 2010; Zlatev et al., 2010; Mey, 1985), and social semiotics (Böck & Pashler, 2013; Kress, 2010, 1993). However, the point tends to erode in day-to-day research practices which are characterized by a rather strict division of labour between system-oriented and processing-oriented approaches to the lexicon and to language research in general (see Hörmann, 1986, for a critical account that largely remains valid today). Given that naming & framing lies at the very crux of these matters, the following account will naturally contribute to the discussion in certain respects, one example being the links established between experimental research into people's real-time decoding and acquisition of familiar and unfamiliar composite names (see Sections 2.3 and 3.2.1) and the theoretical debates on the status of lexical non-arbitrariness (motivation) in language viewed as a conventionalized code (see Sections 2.1 and 2.2), as mediated by theorizing on the situated nature of human categorization (see Section 1.3.2). Such complementary perspectives sometimes do co-occur in more general treatments of the lexicon (Aitchison, 2012; Benczes, 2006), yet there seems to be an unexploited potential for combining them at the operational level when pursuing specific research goals relating to naming, framing, and multimodality (see Sections 2.4 and 3.2.1).

Last but not least, the present focus on naming, and hence words and language, does not exclude but, on the contrary, requires consideration of the role played by other potential carriers of communicative content, also referred to as semiotic modalities: pictures, colours, shapes, physical interaction, and so on. In most communicative settings and the communicative products that emerge from them (news articles, homepages, advertisements, films, university lectures, product packaging, and so on), words are surrounded by elaborate symphonies or "cocktails" of other semiotic resources which demonstrably influence the communicative effect exerted by the words, while the choice of words influences the interpretation of the surrounding nonverbal elements (cf. Powell et al., 2019; Jewitt et al., 2016; Smith, Barratt, & Zlatev, 2014; Kress, 2010; Kress & van Leeuwen, 2001). As Kress (2010: 1) aptly sums up the situation, *"image shows what takes too long to read, and writing names what would be difficult to show. Colour is used to highlight specific aspects of the overall message."* On that background, care has been taken to avoid what Jones (2014: 3) labels a "language-centric" view of goal-driven communication while at the same time accommodating the specifics that words demonstrably do display as elements of the total multimodal mix. The multimodal dimension will be taken up again in Sections 1.2.1 and 2.3 and taken substantially further from Section 3.1 onwards.

As regards the application of the proposed framework to concrete communicative domains and challenges, it should be clear by now that this is not a book about family relations, foreign politics, marketing, health care, food labelling, climate change, or any other particular area of human activity where exercising the power of words is a decisive factor. Rather, it aims at completing the toolbox of researchers and practitioners investigating or engaging in naming & framing processes across a variety of real-life domains while selectively addressing some of them for illustration.

1 Naming & Framing at Level 1

Having a Name for It

1.1 Naming Something Is Having It, but Who's to Decide?

"If you don't have a name for something, then as far as people are concerned, you don't have it at all," states Kevin Tracey in a promotion video for the services of Tracey Communications (Massachusetts, USA).[1] Tracey attributes the point to the semiotician Marshall Blonsky, but it echoes a relatively broad consensus among language theorists the wider implications of which are however eagerly debated as we shall soon see.

Certainly, real-life support for such a claim appears to be available in abundance. It is hard to imagine *HIV* and *AIDS* hitting the headlines in the 1980s and becoming the subject of debates, information campaigns, support lines, charity work, and political decision-making, before these phenomena had not only been identified and described, but also unambiguously named (Emke, 2000; Berridge, 1996; Colby & Cook, 1991). The drastic developments presently evolving around the name *Covid-19* still remain to be fully comprehended and recorded in these respects. In turn, this is what is now happening with the sequence of events known as *Brexit*, a term that gave supporters and opponents of such a political decision in the UK a more tangible target for their campaigning than would a formal phrase like "United Kingdom invocation of Article 50 of the Treaty on European Union." Arguably, the name also came to underpin a less technical conceptualization of the whole matter in the wider British public, leaving essential consequences unattended till later (Smith, 2017; Walsh, 2017).

Another group of examples are what some marketers and product developers term "really new products," i.e. innovations which

---

1 https://traceycommunications.com/?p=579 (accesses June 2020).

require severe conceptual reorganizations in the minds of consumers to be understood and accepted or rejected (Nielsen, Escalas, & Hoeffler, 2018; Charette, Hooker, & Stanton, 2015; Alexander, Lynch, & Wang, 2008; Hoeffler, 2003; Song & Montoya-Weiss, 1998; see also Rogers, 2010 on the acceptance of new social practices and services). A good example are the compact electronic devices that combine the properties of a mobile phone with those of a laptop, a TV set, a camera, a music player, a GPS, and much else (Park & Chen, 2007; for related examples, see Gattol, Sääksjärvi, Gill, & Schoormans, 2016). Agreeing on "a name for it" here became a vital step towards catching consumers' attention, facilitating their understanding of the innovation, and ultimately increasing demands, as accomplished in this case by the name *smartphone* (and *tablet* for larger variants with somewhat different advantages and drawbacks).

At the same time, new names are not always created for labelling entirely new phenomena. They may also categorize and present things that have been around us all along in a new way. For example, people who qualify as *nerds* in present-day English (and e.g. in Danish, Swedish, German, and Russian, with some variations of spelling and pronunciation) are likely to have existed and displayed certain distinct personal characteristics even before that name was invented (otherwise, why invent it?). Likewise, (some) men have surely been explaining complicated matters to women in a patronizing fashion, and many of us have experienced the feeling of being hungry and increasingly angry at the same time before these phenomena were labelled *mansplaining* and *hangry* in English and the words included in the Oxford English Dictionary (OED, 2018). Moreover, whether something qualifies to have a name or not may in itself be subject to debate. For example, the term *premenstrual syndrome* (*PMS*) which dates back to the 1930s has still not been accepted as a valid diagnosis for a distinct medical disorder by many physicians and female citizens (Figert, 2017; Rodin, 1992; see Brown, 1995 on other diagnosis names).

As the examples illustrate, some new names hint at what they are supposed to mean by virtue of their composition and/or origin (e.g. *mansplaining*) while others do not (e.g. *nerd*), which does, however, not make the latter names less comprehensible. The very fact of "having a name for it" thus makes a tremendous difference which is the key point pursued in this chapter. The additional flavour potentially added by the expression-unit chosen for the purpose will be further explored in Chapter 2 (leading us to naming & framing at Level 2).

At this point, another question imposes itself: Are there no limits to what can potentially be provided with a dedicated name? The question is particularly prominent for general names denoting categories of things such as fake news, nerds, or smartphones in that a number of people must agree on identifying these entities by more or less similar criteria and calling them by the same name to ensure successful communication. The case is somewhat different for proper names in that everyone is, in principle, entitled to name their cat or bicycle whatever they like and others will usually recognize and go along with that decision (for an illustrative, though polemical, discussion of the social interaction involved, see Devitt & Sterelny, 1999: 66–82). An intermediate case is posed by brand names like *Apple* and single-referent names like *Brexit* which have certain traits in common with proper names (i.e. the fixed referents), but nevertheless presuppose the existence of a generalized intersubjective content to fulfil their purpose (see e.g. Kaufmann, Loureiro, & Manarioti, 2016; Thomson & Crocker, 2015; Maurya & Mishra, 2012). These specifics will concern us in due course. For now, the overall question is whether everybody can modify the vocabulary of their native language as they see fit, considering that language is a collective construct usually shared by a large body of individuals.

The question echoes a longstanding theoretical debate, or rather two closely connected ones: the opposition between linguistic universalism and linguistic relativism on the one hand, and that between a static and a dynamic understanding of human categorization and its manifestations in language on the other. We will consider them in turn.

1.2 What Language(s) May and Must

According to the universalist view (for some variants and critical discussion, see Pavlenko, 2014; Regier, Kay, Gilbert, & Ivry, 2010; Pinker, 1994; Pinxten, 1976; Fodor, 1975), different languages may well have different lexical and grammatical means for referring to perceived reality, but given that all languages ultimately build upon the same basic cognitive structures, such means can be combined and adapted to express any content required in any language. The opposite view, known as linguistic relativism, ultimately dates back at least to the Bible's tale of the Tower of Babel (BibleGateway, 2011: 11, 1–9); for more recent formulations, see e.g. Bentsen (2018); Durst-Andersen (2011); Deutscher (2010); von Humboldt, 1999 [1836]; Wierzbicka (1997); Baldinger (1980); Whorf (1956). The basic argument is that the world's languages not only reflect, but shape and maintain the way their users understand the world so that each language comes to encapsulate a unique worldview that cannot be transposed to any other language in a 1:1 fashion or altered by its speakers by any short-term measures. The state as such is referred to as linguistic relativity.

For many years, the debates centred around fundamental theoretical positions rather than in-depth analyses of larger portions of linguistic data, relying on isolated (and disputed) examples such as Eskimo languages allegedly having more than 100 words for snow (usually relying on Boas, 1911: 25–26, who however only mentions four) or Hopi Indians having no expressions for time (Whorf, 1956: 57). However, during the last 3–4 decades, more systematic investigations targeting a larger number of languages and semantic domains have been conducted, uncovering a number of generalizable typological differences which divide even closely related languages such as the Indo-European. Focus areas include the lexical and/or grammatical means available for referring to space and motion, different types of physical objects, colours, numbers, cultural stereotypes, and others (Koster & Cadierno, 2018; Groh, 2016; Korzen, 2016; Durst-Andersen, 2011; Tse & Altarriba, 2008; Slobin, 2004; Talmy, 2000: 23–146; Wierzbicka, 1997; Hardin & Maffi, 1997; Berlin & Kay, 1969).

Moreover, it has been suggested that some of the general trends observed correlate with certain cultural and structural specifics of the societies in which the languages are spoken. This reasoning has been applied to areas as diverse as the divide between common-law and civil-law legal thinking (Legrand, 1997a, b) and the precise understanding of society-bound notions such as freedom and friendship (Wierzbicka, 1997). It has furthermore been assessed on experimental grounds whether language-typological differences influence the performance of the native speakers of different languages on tasks that go beyond expressing a given content through language such as natural-scene perception and recall and categorization of events in film clips or crime accounts (Rojo & Cifuentes-Férez, 2017; Berthele & Stocker, 2016; Malt, Gennari, & Imai, 2010; Papafragou, Massey, & Gleitman, 2002). The results are not unequivocal, but they do seem to provide support for the overall idea in certain respects.

All of this has led some authors to propose a "weak" version of linguistic relativism, arguing that while language structure alone cannot determine people's worldview in every respect, it may still direct their attention to different aspects of otherwise comparable objects and phenomena, especially when it comes to putting their thoughts into words, i.e. "thinking for speaking" (Slobin, 1996; see also Kone, 2013; Deutscher, 2010; Gumperz & Levinson, 1996). Virtually the same point was anticipated years earlier by Jakobson in the following subtle passage: "Languages differ essentially in what they *must* convey, not in what they *may* convey" (1959: 236).

To take a simple example: The English word *ball* corresponds to two words in French, namely *balle* or *ballon*, depending on the object's size. This is in line with the more general observation that the Romance languages (here: French) tend to have a more varied core vocabulary for human artefacts, differentiating them by their immediate visual appearance, whereas the Germanic languages (here: English) tend to operate with fewer basic nouns (word roots) labelling the objects in accordance with their functional properties (e.g. the ability to roll). Another example would be the Danish word *kande* (≈ 'jug') which corresponds to *brocca, bricco, caraffa, annaffiatoio*, and more in Italian depending on materials and shape (for further examples and discussion, see Korzen, 2006; Herslund & Baron, 2003; Legrand, 1997b: 56–57).

However, such tendencies do not prevent English and French speakers from giving dedicated names to whatever subtypes of (what is in English called) balls they see as sufficiently communicatively and cognitively important, e.g. by creating composite names such as the English *tennis ball* and *basketball (ball)* and correspondingly *balle de tennis* and *ballon de basket* in French (i.e. secondary lexicalizations based on re-use of the primary lexicalizations available in the language in question, cf. Smith, 2000). Only, the different starting points in terms of relevant head noun mean that the French names come to explicitly stress the difference in size which the English do not.

Certainly, few English speakers would probably need to have that information spelled out for them in the first place. Yet, a risk of miscommunication may nevertheless occur, for instance, if an English native speaker only superficially familiar with French encounters less typical combinations such as *ballon de tennis* and *balle de basket* – say, when used *ad hoc* for referring to an oversized tennis ball suitable as a dog toy and a miniature basketball intended for decoration; see Figure 1.1a and b.

Without having access to multimodal contexts such as those shown in Figure 1.1a and b that combine both visual and verbal cues, the English speaker would be unlikely to get the twist, and

16 Naming & Framing at Level 1

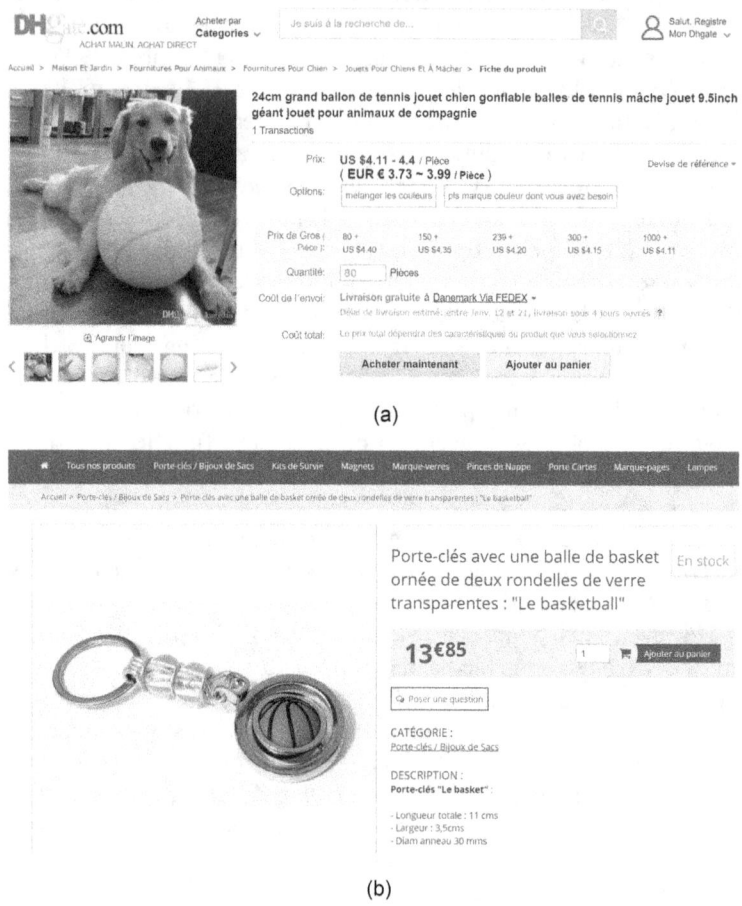

Figure 1.1 Non-typical uses of the French words *balle* and *ballon* in composite names denoting non-typical referents in terms of size, as found in e-store product descriptions. (a) The name *ballon de tennis* referring to an oversized tennis ball in DHGate.com. (b) The name *balle de basked* referring to a miniature basketball in Home-Créa.

explaining it would require more words in English than in French. Notably, while example *b* is taken from an original French homepage,[2] example *a* is taken from the homepage of a Chinese-owned

---
2 https://homecrea.eproshopping.fr/ (accessed June 2020).

e-commerce company offering its goods and services across a vast number of countries and languages,[3] which means that the French wording is most likely the result of a (in this case contextually adequate) creative translation.

In other cases, the content encoded *a priori* into the lexical building blocks available in a given language may, however, be the cause of severe miscommunication when content originally articulated in one language is transposed into another language. This has, for instance, been demonstrated for numeric and colour terms used for reproducing foreign product and brand names in Mandarin Chinese due to the formal, semantic, and cultural specifics of these word elements (Chang & Lii, 2008; Chan & Huang, 2001; Ang, 1997); for further discussion and examples of some unfortunate cross-linguistic transpositions, see Section 2.4. Even so, a suitable name can usually be found.

In sum, the historically developed idiosyncrasies of any given language may indeed exert a certain influence on what qualifies to have a name *a priori*, and on which features are foregrounded by the name. But language users in all societies still adapt their lexicon in accordance with their current cognitive and communicative needs which are determined by many other factors than such long-term language-internal influences; these are further discussed in Chapters 3 and 4. Language-internal factors may nevertheless still exert some influence on what the resultant names come to "say" literally (i.e. on naming & framing at Level 2, see Table 0.1 and Chapter 2); yet, factors such as spontaneous creativity, situational adequacy, personal preferences, and sometimes conscious strategic and persuasive considerations seem to play an equally important role here. For example, the composition of English names such as *sex worker* and *crowd funding* hardly comes down to the language-typological characteristics of English alone (though the choice of a noun-noun compound rather than, say, a derivation or a phrasal lexeme which is more frequent in other languages than English probably does). In any case, communicators do wisely in working with rather than against the typological preferences of the language(s) in which they operate, while bearing in mind that this is not the only factor that determines the acceptance and success of a lexical innovation.

---

3 https://www.dhgate.com/ (accessed June 2020).

1.3 From ad-hoc Categories to First Candidates for Naming

Returning to *what* can successfully be provided with a dedicated name, the main precondition thus still seems to be that at least some people apart from the person who invented the name experience a cognitive and communicative need for it and that they can agree more or less on what the name means. How does such a consensus come about?

As indicated in Section 0.3, the present book takes a cognitivist approach to human language in seeing it as both based on and affecting other kinds of cognitive functions. The latter includes the (evolutionarily more ancient) function of *categorization*, i.e. the ability to distinguish entities of one kind from entities of all other kinds by applying criteria that go beyond pure instinct. Advanced animals also have that ability in that, say, a dog (on a good day) is able to distinguish its toys from its owner's shoes and (most certainly) activities that it likes to engage in from those it resents (though the wider theoretical implications of such observations are subject to eager debate, see e.g. Smith, Zakrzewski, Johnson, Valleau, & Church, 2016; Newen & Bartels, 2007; Tomasello, 2003). Still, humans take this capability substantially further in distinguishing (more or less) clearly between smartphones and dumbphones, assistant professors and associate professors, blind dates and job interviews, and so on. Moreover, they may assign a single name to all members of each such category instead of naming them individually, thereby enabling generalized verbal communication about them and fixing them in their collective memory.

In line with the predominant view in cognitively oriented language theory (Ramscar & Port, 2015; Geeraerts, 2010; Evans & Green, 2006; Jackendoff, 1990; Lakoff, 1987; Wierzbicka, 1985), we classify the mental entities that support such categorizations as *concepts* which could be described as "mental checklists" that comprise the totality of criteria that people use for singling out and qualifying whatever they need to categorize. Notably, the cognitive function of concepts is not restricted to supporting language-based communication – it is just as crucial for nonverbalized thinking and acting. For example, one may notice that an extra chair is needed in a crowded meeting room, and one may go out and fetch one from a neighbouring office (and not necessarily one that looks exactly like the ones in the meeting room, as long as you can sit on it), without hearing or saying the word *chair* at any point. However, if a category becomes sufficiently important to a sufficient number of people, the corresponding concept may ultimately be provided with an intersubjectively accepted unit of permanent lexical expression, i.e. lexicalized, and hence (also) be enrolled into the language that these people speak, in which capacity it is said to function as the *meaning* of the corresponding expression-unit.[4] We will return to the establishment of this link shortly. First, we need to take a closer look at the internal structure of human concepts and how it can be modelled.

1.3.1 The Anatomy of Human Concepts

Rather than describing concepts as linear arrays of mutually independent criteria (components, features, markers, predicates, etc.) as is commonplace in many pre-cognitive linguistic and philosophical accounts, they are here understood as complex graded structures that reflect the subjectivity and fuzzy boundaries of human categorization (Murphy, 2010; Barsalou, 1987; Lakoff, 1987). These criteria (components) may be subdivided into:

a *essential components* which correspond to properties that any entity must possess in order to be accepted as belonging to the category in question, e.g. our expectation that a smartphone must be able to go online;

b *prototypical components* which correspond to properties that are a central part of our understanding of the category as a whole, but must not necessarily apply to every particular exemplar, e.g. our expectation that smartphones mostly have touchscreens, though some may have buttons, or that they are usually more expensive than dumbphones.

---

4 At least, such a 1:1 identification of cognitive and linguistic variables is feasible for the meaning of nouns which denote "things" in the widest sense the identification and categorization of which appear to be pivotal on both the cognitive and the linguistic levels. The case is somewhat more complex for verbs which lexicalize (generalized mental models of) situations the various elements of which may be conflated differently by the default lexicalization patterns found in different languages – take *walk/drive/fly/sail out* in English versus *sortir* in French. Specifying the manner of motion is thus optional in the latter case, which, on the other hand, does not exclude that it may be specified if so wished by additional lexical means. For further details and theoretical implications, see Durst-Andersen, Smith, & Thomsen (2013); Slobin (2004); Herslund & Baron (2003); Talmy (2000).

20 Naming & Framing at Level 1

For components at both levels, an additional distinction[5] can be made between:

a *sensory components* which rely on immediate recall of first-order sensory experiences, e.g. the experience of seeing, touching, and using a genuine smartphone;
b *propositional components* which involve factual second-order knowledge potentially susceptible to truth-conditional evaluation, e.g. knowing that smartphones must contain a central processing unit (CPU) and analogue-digital and digital-analogue (AD and DA) converters in order to operate. We will return to the essential circumstance that many users of smartphones lack the latter kind of knowledge in Section 3.3.

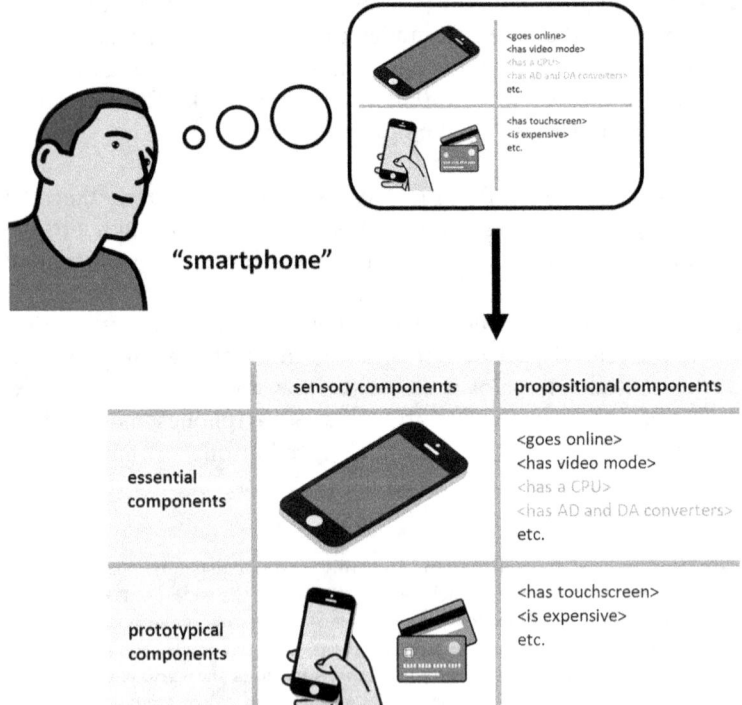

Figure 1.2 Componential analysis of the concept conveyed by the name *smartphone*.

5 Another way of capturing the same key point is to describe human concepts a synthesis of an "image" and an "idea" which mutually presuppose each other and together make up an image-idea pair (Durst-Andersen, 2011: 132–144).

The key distinctions introduced earlier are summarized in Figure 1.2. More details on the grey-toned elements follow in Section 3.3. For additional details on the theorizing, evidence, and debates underlying the present account (and some of the theoretical and terminological variations bridged by it), see Barsalou (2016; 1987); Murphy (2010, 2004); Patterson, Nestor, & Rogers (2007); Geeraerts (2006); Wierzbicka (1985); Rosch (1975); Smith, Shoben, & Rips (1974); Zadeh (1965).

1.3.2 *A Dynamic Approach to Human Categorization*

Most classic accounts of human categorization tacitly assume that concepts are static entities that are permanently present in the mind of anyone who "has" the concept in question. Moreover, the very identification and delimitation of concepts is often linked with the existence of "a word for them," thereby rendering the distinction between concepts and meanings somewhat tautological, despite claims to the contrary; the strong formulation of linguistic relativism mentioned earlier is but one example of this (for critical discussion, see e.g. Ramscar & Port, 2015; Zlatev & Blomberg, 2015; Malt & Wolff, 2010). However, this reasoning has been increasingly challenged, most consistently by Barsalou (2016, 2010, 2003, 1995, 1987, 1983; see also Wyer & Srull, 2014; Kiefer & Barsalou, 2013; Murphy, 2010; Wilson & Carston, 2007; Kurtz & Gentner, 2001).

In an early work, Barsalou summarizes his point as follows: "Rather than being retrieved as static units from memory to represent categories, concepts originate in a highly flexible process that retrieves generic and episodic information from long-term memory to construct temporary concepts in working memory" (1987: 101). Stated differently, whenever we need to distinguish something from something else, while also qualifying it in various respects, we draw on the total pool of knowledge and experiences available to us and retrieve the set of criteria (components) needed for the purpose. The analysis extends both to:

a   categories established for sheer ad-hoc purposes such as distinguishing things that one needs to take on an upcoming camping trip from things that one does not (necessarily) need to take, or food products that are compatible with one's low-carb diet from products that are not (or less) compatible, and

b   categories that are (re)identified on a regular basis by a larger number of individuals because they repeatedly turn out to be crucial to their interaction with their environment (e.g. friends, smartphones, chairs, and faculty meetings).

Importantly, the concepts that support the respective categorizations appear to be structured according to same basic patterns in both cases (as shown in Figure 1.2). Thus, a similar analysis could be applied to the camping-trip and the low-carb-diet examples.

However, there is a marked difference when it comes to means of linguistic expression. While concepts for ad-hoc categories usually have to be conveyed by longer paraphrases such as "things I need for my camping trip" (or possibly idiosyncratic ad-hoc names such as *my camping stuff*), concepts for more stable categories will prototypically have been provided with a permanent lexical expression, i.e. lexicalized. We will here refer to the latter entities as *salient concepts* (see also e.g. Liu, Chin, & Ng, 2003), while Barsalou primarily speaks of concepts for permanent categories while stressing the essential reservations to "permanent" just explained. Some concepts will be salient with most people on earth, others will be restricted to particular societies and/or cultures, and yet others to specific subgroups within and across them. For example, *Thanksgiving dinner* lexicalizes a concept which is salient with most US Americans but relatively few people outside the USA, whereas *water hammer* lexicalizes a concept which is salient with plumbers and water engineers across the globe but not too many other people (for technical details, see e.g. Ghidaoui, Zhao, McInnis, & Axworthy, 2005), as also expressed by *trykstød* (lit. ≈ 'pressure push') in Danish, *coup de belier* (lit. ≈ 'ram's stroke') in French, and гидроудар (lit. ≈ 'hydro blow') in Russian.

The different ways in which the latter names present (frame) the concept in question relate to naming & framing at Level 2, as further discussed in Sections 2.1–2.4. What should be noted here, however, is that the concept must necessarily have grown salient with the relevant groups of people even before the respective names were created (otherwise, why create them?) which, in turn, entails that many essential and prototypical conceptual components will remain the same across all "local versions" of the concept, quite independently of the names chosen. Another way of stating this point (following Smith, 2000) is that the *what*-aspect of lexicalization needs to be distinguished from the *how*-aspect of lexicalization, but that the former at the same time cannot simply be reduced to a naïve realist idea of the referents already "being out there" and language merely providing labels for them (for a critical overview of some lines of theorizing largely following the latter path, see Devitt & Sterelny, 1999: 83–113).[6] As the examples illustrate, the situation is usually more complex than that: First, "it" must be crystallized cognitively which is already a non-trivial task, then a name must be provided and in some cases the name collectively agreed on may add some shades to the semantics of its own.

Importantly, none of this excludes that potential candidates for receiving a name may already be "out there" independently of human cognition, not least in the case of so-called natural kinds for which it can be argued that they fall under a particular category by virtue of certain nature-given properties, e.g. water, bananas, cats, dogs, earthquakes, and red blood cells (though some proponents of social constructivism may well disagree and/or reject the question as irrelevant; see Roberts-Miller, 2002 for further discussion). Rather, the point is that it takes a human mind (and brain) and a shared language to (try to) identify such entities and communicate about them. For example, it is hard to imagine that red blood cells or Alzheimer's disease could be subsumed under well-delimited categories and referred to by precise names in the year of 1659, even if the phenomena denoted by these terms today

---

6 Devitt & Sterelny (1999: 83–113) offer an illustrative yet (self-)critical account of so-called causal theories of reference which rely extensively on ostensive definitions, i.e. on the assumption that tangible objects such as cats or gold have originally been physically pointed out and named by some "dubber" and that others have borrowed that reference by observing the use of the name in similar situations. The declared meta-theoretical goal, at least in earlier formulations of this approach, was to eliminate the need for referring to concepts, thoughts, and other "troublesome" cognitive variables to explain word meaning. However, despite its clear virtues in highlighting the pivotal role of immediate sensory cues in word acquisition (see also Sections 2.3 and 3.1), the argument leaves several other key questions unanswered as captured by the examples *red blood cells* and *Alzheimer's disease* in the main text. This too is readily recognized and vividly illustrated by the present authors, yet without pointing out any preferable alternatives. However, both the causal paradigm and the closely related approach of Putnam (1975a) addressed in Section 3.3 are open to cognitive (re)interpretations on their own terms (as shown also by e.g. Keil, Stein, Webb, Billings, & Rozenblit, 2008; Geeraerts, 2006; Durst-Andersen, 1992; Lakoff, 1987) and in that case they add essential new shades to our understanding of the role of interpersonal interaction in the genesis of conventionalized word meaning(s). One essential implication of this is taken further in Section 3.3 with specific reference to Putnam's (1975) hypothesis of division of linguistic labour.

are likely to have existed even then. The need to (also) include cognitive variables such as knowledge and concepts to fully explain the language-reality interface becomes even more evident for socially and culturally still deeper embedded categories such as associate professors, fake news, and water hammers: It takes more than pointing out an associate professor or a piece of fake news "out there" to know what qualifies them for the title and to recognize the next instance encountered.

On this background, the key precondition for successfully introducing a new (general) name in a given language can be narrowed down to the existence of a *salient concept* in the relevant population for whatever it lexicalizes. However, such an understanding also entails a methodological challenge: How do we identify concepts and assess their internal structure and situational or general salience independently of the lexical expressions that they may or may not (yet) have been provided with? Without going into extensive methodological details in the present work, it should be noted that such methods have indeed been developed and are routinely applied in some fields.

In knowledge engineering and terminology management, for instance, methods have been developed for bottom-up extraction and modelling of conceptual structures (ontologies) from text corpora, expert interviews, informants' performance in category-generation and item-sorting tasks, and other indicators of structured conceptual knowledge (Ribeiro & Cerveira, 2018; Madsen & Thomsen, 2015; Pinto & Martins, 2004; Liu et al., 2003; Kim, Suh, & Hwang, 2003; Ross & Murphy, 1999). Taking a more behaviour-oriented perspective, marketers and consumer psychologists have furthermore mapped consumers' establishment of goal-derived categories in simulated decision-making situations while pursuing set goals such as buying food for a healthy breakfast or a long car drive (Huh, Vosgerau, & Morewedge, 2016; Nguyen & McCullough, 2009; Shocker, Bayus, & Kim, 2004; Ratneshwar, Barsalou, Pechmann, & Moore, 2001). In future research, the applicability of such methodologies might be tested also relative to other domains, say, voters' and medias' categorization of political agendas or alternative ways of supporting climate sustainability, thereby supplementing insights gained thorough established methods such as text and discourse analysis (Poberezhskaya & Ashe, 2018; Drews & van den Bergh, 2016; Klüver & Sagarzaz, 2016).

However, while being a necessary precondition for lexicalization, conceptual salience is not per definition a sufficient one. The dynamic character of both cognition and language appears to leave room for a "grey zone." As already mentioned, the typological preferences of individual languages may thus put different sorts of information "first in line" to become unambiguously lexicalized, as we saw it with the naming of round objects in English versus French in Section 1.2. Moreover, even if a concept has grown salient with a group of individuals who speak the same language, it may take a while before someone suggests a name for expressing it – if that happens at all. The degree of everyday communicative importance also seems to be a factor here. The inclusion of *mansplaining* and *hangry* in the Oxford English Dictionary mentioned earlier may serve as a perhaps somewhat anecdotic illustration of such "grey zone" cases. Less anecdotic examples are *deep state* and *fake news* which, indeed, seem to have filled essential gaps in current socio-political debates.

1.4 Success Criteria for Naming at Level 1 Revisited

The total picture is therefore something like this: Chances of successfully introducing a new name in a given language are good if the cognitive ground has already been prepared by the salience of a corresponding concept in (parts of) the relevant population. In that case, not too many additional cues will be required from the built-in semantic potential of the name itself (i.e. naming & framing at Level 2) and from the way the name is framed by other words and nonverbal cues in running communication (i.e. naming & framing at Level 3) for people to understand the name as intended and start spreading it further. By contrast, names for completely new objects and phenomena (or ways of seeing them) cannot be expected to match a concept that is salient with too many people in advance. And yet, this is precisely the scenario, say, when a company introduces an innovative product (as smartphones and tablets were once) or researchers suggest a new theoretical paradigm. In such cases, the concept must gradually be "made" salient with still more people in parallel with exposing them to the name. This poses different demands both to the choice of name (at Level 2) and to its framing in running communication (at Level 3) as further discussed in the chapters to follow.

Before proceeding, it needs a brief mention that the successful introduction of a name for something does not automatically imply that people will agree on its meaning in every respect. People may have different opinions on such matters as what makes a company a genuine *startup* or a fruit drink a genuine *smoothie* which indicates that the conceptual structures that these people connect with the names are not entirely identical. This perspective is addressed in further depth in Section 3.3. At present, the simple point is that the provision of "a name for it" is still the first precondition for any such variations and negotiations of meaning becoming possible in the first place.

2 Naming & Framing at Level 2
The Joyce Principle

2.1 Juliet's Wisdom versus Joyce's Creativity

One thing is "having a name for it"; another is how the choice of name may affect people's understanding of "it" and how they get to agree on what exactly "it" is and what it means to them. In an illustrative account focusing primarily on brand and product naming while being largely unknown beyond the realm of marketing, Collins (1977) suggests a set of terms that rather aptly captures the essence of these two perspectives: the *Joyce principle* and the *Juliet principle*. The same basic issues have been addressed in further depth in other disciplines, but not as aptly named. We will therefore consider Collins's point first.

Collins first establishes the Juliet principle, as encapsulated in the following much-quoted line from William Shakespeare's play Romeo and Juliet (2010 [1597]): "*Juliet:* What's in a name? That which we call a rose by any other word would smell as sweet; so Romeo would, were he not Romeo call'd, retain that dear perfection which he owes without that title." In other words, the name does not matter, the important thing is what it denotes and what we think and say about it. In principle, a *sandwich* might just as well have been called a *cardigan* in English and vice versa (to use Collins's examples) which would have no bearing on their meaning. Likewise, brand names such as *Kellogg's* and *Reebok* do not in themselves say anything about cereals or sports; that link is established through the brand communication surrounding the names only.

However, names like *Whumies* or *British Bakeries* are different in that respect. Though one could hardly predict the exact content of such names without knowing it already, their etymology and/or composition (which may also include their sound structure) strongly suggest that they could not mean just anything. Collins here refers to the Joyce principle, hinting at the use of self-created suggestive words in the literary work of James Joyce. However, rather than discussing which principle is the "right" one (a longstanding debate reaching far beyond marketing, see below), Collins's approach has become a catalyst for presuming a coexistence of both principles and for addressing the possible interplay between them in strategic naming & framing processes (Muzellec, 2006; Riezebos, Kist, & Kootstra, 2003: 51ff; Usunier & Shaner, 2002). In the following, we take this line of reasoning further, beginning with the Joyce principle (corresponding to Level 2 of naming & framing in Table 0.1) and continuing with the Juliet principle (corresponding to Level 3 of naming & framing in Table 0.1) in the next chapter.

2.2 Limits to Lexical Arbitrariness: Names Talk!

A just indicated, Collins's study mirrors a much broader debate. In traditional and, in particular, structural language theory, it remains a widespread assumption that the link between a word in itself (viewed as a string of sounds or written characters) and what it means is a matter of sheer convention, that is, completely *arbitrary* (Saussure, 2011 [1916]; Lyons, 1977: 70ff; Hockett, 1958; Hjelmslev, 1953 [1943]). This may make good sense for *sandwich* and *cardigan* (if one is unaware of the etymological prehistory that these names actually do have) and even better sense for simple singe-root words such as *cow, leg,* or *love,* that simply "mean what they mean." However, the majority of names found in developed languages are not quite as arbitrary. As Langacker (1987: 12) bluntly states it, "the arbitrary character of the linguistic sign is easily overstated, despite the important kernel of truth in the principle of l'arbitraire du signe." For English, the list of such "Joyce-principle names" could thus easily be continued by e.g. *crash, smoothie, bug* (the malware), *startup* (the company type), *blueberry, monkey wrench, deep state, range anxiety, managed democracy, red light district, Burger King,* and *Whopper.*

Linguists and semioticians who acknowledge the additional semantic complexity of such examples refer to them as *non-arbitrary* or *motivated* in one way or the other (Marzo, 2015; Kress, 2010; 1993; Nöth, 1995: 240–256; Waugh, 1993; Ullmann, 1962; Wüster, 1959/1960). We will here resort to Ullmann's (1962: 81–93) classic classification of different types of lexical motivation which adds essential details to Collins's illustrative but somewhat sketchy account on this point:

- **Phonetic motivation** based on a sense of iconic or symbolic connection between the sound structure of the name and what it denotes, e.g. *boom, crash, smoothie, Yahoo*. A related case could be made for *graphic motivation* (though this aspect is not taken up by Ullman) in particular for product and brand names where the choice of fonts, colours, surrounding imagery, etc., may become an intrinsic part of the name's expectable appearance and support certain expectations in their own right; take *Coca Cola* or *Burger King* (cf. Klimchuk & Krasovec, 2013: 64–104; Lee & Ang, 2003).

- *Morphological motivation* which emerges when a name is composed of smaller units (morphemes, words) which have a meaning of their own that jointly hint at the meaning of the whole name. If we constrain our focus to the Indo-European languages, the predominant patterns (while unevenly distributed across these languages) are affixation, compounding, and the formation of phrasal lexemes, as illustrated by English names such as *gamer, radicalization, clickbait, sleep hygiene, Me Too*, and *Michael Learns to Rock* (the band).
- *Semantic motivation* where a new meaning is attached to an existing name on the basis of a meaning it already had, usually relying on metaphor or metonymy of some sort, e.g. (computer) *cookie, house* (the music style), *Apple* (the brand name), and so on.

More than one type of motivation will often have contributed at different stages of the formation of a given name, e.g. *Baby Boomers*.

The wider implications of these observations have however not as yet been exhaustively explored. While the formal aspects of word formation have received substantial attention in the linguistic literature (for a comprehensive overview, see Müller, Ohnheiser, Olsen, & Rainer, 2015), the semantic and cognitive consequences of choosing one word formation pattern in preference to another for naming something specific have been less systematically addressed, leaving essential issues open to debate (Marzo, 2015; Libben, 2014; Smith, Barratt, & Zlatev, 2014; Waugh, 1993; Lyons, 1977: 534–550). Notably, this includes the degree to which any underlying motivation matters at all once the name has been generally accepted. In other words, even if some names "talk" more than others, there is no guarantee that people will feel obliged to listen.

Ultimately, lexical non-arbitrariness can be described as a simple side effect of the circumstance that the demand for new words is ever increasing, while the crystallization of new, truly arbitrary lexical expression-units (word roots) in organically evolving languages proceeds at a very slow pace. This renders re-use and re-organization of existing linguistic resources as the primary sources of lexical innovation, as manifest in the archetypical patterns just presented (Sager, 1990: 55–90). However, creating new names on these grounds is bound to influence the full communicative potential of the resultant expression-unit in essential respects. Moreover, that potential is demonstrably being exploited by strategically minded communicators for pursuing specific communicative goals, whether fully aware of the underlying linguistic and cognitive mechanisms or not.

To take a few examples. Problems with sleeping and ways of dealing with them have been recognized for ages. Yet, the term *sleep hygiene* has consolidated this issue as a distinct medical field, not only by providing a compact heading for research and practices (Irish, Kline, Gunn, Buysse, & Hall, 2015; Stepanski & Wyatt, 2003; Brown, Buboltz, & Soper, 2002), but also by transposing certain key properties of hygiene in the traditional sense to a new field (also known as property mapping, cf. Swaminathan, Gürhan-Canli, Kubat, & Hayran, 2015; Wisniewski, 1996). Likewise, while the idea of using taxation to support environmental policies has a long prehistory, names such as *ecotax* and *green tax* have contributed to qualifying this agenda in a readily comprehensible and, at least to some people, appealing way (Drews & van den Bergh, 2016; Backhaus, 1999). Transposed to the analysis of conceptual structure given in Section 1.3.1 (Figure 1.2), the name highlights specific essential and/or prototypical components of the underlying (already salient) concept and may also add new ones that would not necessarily have been part of the concept otherwise, for instance, a direct linkage between environmental concerns and the concept of ecology.

Turning from morphological to semantic motivation, the word *bubble* has recently been relaunched as a name for an intellectual state where a person only seeks and receives (especially online) information that is consistent with his or her pre-established beliefs and values (as first suggested by Pariser, 2011; see also Nguyen, Hui, Harper, Terveen, & Konstan, 2014; Resnick, Garrett, Kriplean, Munson, & Stroud, 2013). Here, the metaphorical potential of *bubble* contributes to highlighting both the hermetically closed nature of the condition and its potential for bursting, or deliberately being burst (for further discussion on the persuasive power of metaphors, see Charteris-Black, 2011; Handl & Schmid, 2011; Fairhurst & Sarr, 1996; Lakoff, 1987: 377–585). Finally, the auditive appeal of product names such as *slush ice* and brand names such as *Yahoo* has long been subject to explicit attention in marketing research encouraging companies to supplement sheer intuition with more systematic pre-testing in that regard (Sidhu & Pexman, 2018; Krishna, 2012; Shrum & Lowrey, 2007; Klink, 2001).

A special case is posed by deliberate efforts to *rename* objects or events that are already covered by an existing name, at least as far as denotation is concerned, by introducing a substitute name. For example, the name *sex worker* (Jackson, 2016; Levy & Jakobsson, 2014) has been suggested as an alternative to *prostitute* (and overlapping terms) for conveying some of the same conceptual components, while also adding new ones that entail greater societal legitimacy.[1] Compositionally, this is backed up by establishing a link to the conventional meaning of *worker*. However, the inclusion of that very element has also led to severe criticism from other interested parties who see it as a way of legitimizing brothel-keeping (Banyard, 2016). The latter circumstance illustrates that the composition of a name can never ensure the intended reading by itself, only in combination with surrounding contextual cues, i.e. the Juliet principle, as further discussed in Chapter 3. But it can definitely give a push.

Another example is *information war* which according to some analysts has been adopted by Russian politicians as a substitute for the more peacefully sounding term *strategic communications* (in the specific military sense) to promote a more aggressive (re)conceptualization of NATO's strategic intentions (Thomas, 2015). However, other authors use the former name in a broader sense, referring to a type of warfare which is gaining still greater significance across the globe (Klein, 2018; Grinyaev, 2001; Molander, Riddile, Wilson, & Williamson, 1996). Again, the choice of name highlights different conceptual components of, in other respects, closely related concepts, entailing different checks and balances between legitimate goals and means. Stated differently, we witness a battle for definitional power over what Gallie (1955) labels essentially contested concepts (see Section 3.3) where the choice of name has in this case become an integrated part of the game.

---

[1] It could be argued that to the wordmaker this is not just a matter of modifying an existing concept, but of lexicalizing a whole new concept that has grown salient with the group in question, even if it happens to overlap with an already lexicalized one in terms of extension (category members) if not intension (categorization criteria). By creating a new name, the carriers/proponents of the new concept will thus invite other people to *re*conceptualize their own understanding of the individuals in question from scratch.

Not all non-arbitrary names seem equally well chosen for their purpose, however. For example, it has been argued that the choice of name was a major reason why a (somewhat hastily conceived) proposal by the Danish government to establish a *betalingsring* (lit. ≈ 'payment ring') around central Copenhagen to reduce car traffic ended up as a complete failure in 2012 (for a recapitulation of the events in English, see Birkbak, 2017). In comparison, a similar arrangement labelled *congestion charge* has been quite successful for several years in London (Leape, 2006). During the preparation of the Danish proposal, the extra tax revenues (i.e. the payment aspect) were indeed a major consideration for the politicians involved, but it was wisely decided to foreground environmental concerns as the main political motivation. However, what was on top of the politicians' minds nevertheless somehow slipped into the name first used in public, and that name was immediately taken over by the media and came to dominate the whole public debate in a negative, obstacle-oriented direction. Subsequent attempts to reframe the issue by speaking of *miljøring* (lit. ≈ 'ecoring'), *trængselsring* (lit. ≈ 'congestion ring'), and *trafikring* (lit. ≈ 'traffic ring') did not make much of a difference. The harm had already been done.

Paradoxically, other names may carry a motivation which is just as poorly balanced with key elements of the intended content – or make little or no sense to a majority of language users in the first place – but still fulfil their purpose very well. For example, the business term *startup* says nothing about attributes such as innovative business idea, fast growth, scalability, or orientation towards resale, but would rather seem to apply to any newly started business. And yet, a concept (and hype) involving precisely such factors has successfully evolved around the name (even if different weight is attributed to each of them by different authors, e.g. Blank & Dorf, 2012; Ries, 2011; see also Section 3.3). Likewise, many speakers of ordinary English are capable of buying *Brussels sprouts* for dinner, operating an *Apple* computer, or even finding a *monkey wrench* in their toolbox without having any idea of why they are so called. Collins's examples *sandwich* and *cardigan* illustrate the same point. Importantly, people may well still conceive these names as motivated in one way or another, but the Juliet principle seems to have taken over completely from the Joyce principle when it comes to ensuring a shared understanding. How come?

2.3 Additional Leads from Language Processing

Essential leads to understanding the mechanisms in play here may be found in the otherwise somewhat insular field of experimental psychology and psycholinguistics investigating people's spontaneous decoding of (what we here call) non-arbitrary names, with a major focus on composite names, in particular, noun-noun compounds (Juhasz, 2018; Schäfer, 2018; Schmidtke, Matsuki, & Kuperman, 2017; Libben, 2014; Aitchison, 2012: 145–168; Gill & Dubé, 2007; Libben & Jarema, 2006; Krott & Nicoladis, 2005; Andrews & Davis, 1999; Ryder, 1994; Sandra, 1990; Manelis & Tharp, 1977).

The results and their interpretation are subject to continuous debate, but the general picture seems to be that we do not routinely split up familiar compounds such as *butter cookie* or *Brussels sprout* in order to establish a meaningful connection between the constituents, but automatically retrieve the full-word meaning that we have acquired at an earlier stage (even if the constituents may still play a certain role in word recognition without affecting whole-word semantics). By contrast, such an additional semantic processing will always take place when people encounter an unfamiliar compound such as *bird phone* or *train juice* (examples taken from Gill & Dubé, 2007) as indicated by longer response latencies in word-decision and other experimental tasks. Here, the recipient is left to extract some immediate sense from the structurally implied but underdetermined statement '(it's some kind of) X [e.g. phone, juice] that is somehow related to (some kind of) Y [e.g. birds, trains]' by inferring additional information at his or her own risk. The process is supported by factors such as the compatibility of the concepts conveyed by the constituents (Lynott & Connell, 2010; Ran & Duimering, 2010; Gagné & Spalding, 2006), frequency-based analogies with familiar complex words containing the same constituents (Krott, 2009; Bybee, 2007, 1995; Krott & Nicoladis, 2005), reliance on recurrent functional patterns and schemas (Goldberg, 2006; Ryder, 1994), and contextual cues if such are available (Zlatev, Smith, van de Weijer, & Skydsgaard, 2010; Gagné, Spaling, & Gorrie, 2005; Mori & Nagy, 1999),[2] as matched against general world knowledge and common sense.

---

[2] Unlike the other factors mentioned, the role of context has so far received relatively limited attention in the mainstream experimental literature on this topic. This can be reasonably explained by a wish to ensure experimental

Notably, while the procedures just described best qualify as instances of situational (pragmatic) inference-making rather than the retrieval of a pre-determined (semantic) meaning, they may also be a first step towards crystallizing such a more permanent (semantic) meaning that people will come to connect with the novel compound regardless of the situation as further argued below (see also Smith, Barratt, & Zlatev, 2014; Zlatev et al., 2010). This is in line with Ariel's (2010: 271–274) proposal to understand code and inference as two modes of sense-making displaying a permanent division of labour with each other rather than as functionally separate levels of decoding. In turn, that aligns with the general observation that language in its capacity as a conventionalized system or code ("langue") is not only generated, but constantly adjusted and expanded in the actual communicative behaviour ("parole") of concrete individuals on concrete occasions as anticipated in Section 0.3.

Of course, even for familiar compounds, people do sometimes stop and reflect on matters such as "why are butter cookies called *butter cookies*?" or "do *Brussel sprouts* really come from Brussels?" (as indicated by the dotted circle in Figure 2.1a), a phenomenon known as metalinguistic reflection (Simard, 2004). However, an appropriate answer to such questions is not decisive for mutual understanding. More vitally, it has been demonstrated that if a familiar compound is presented in a sufficiently biased context (i.e. framing at Level 3), the recipient may be compelled to decompose and *re*-interpret the compound, for example, to understand *bug spray* as a spray produced by bugs (not for killing bugs) or *Hawaiian pizza*[3] as referring to a (frozen) product actually imported from Hawaii (cf. Gagné et al., 2005 and Smith et al., 2014, respectively). In these experiments, the effects were brought about by the surrounding

---

control by excluding all non-mandatory and potentially confounding variables. However, it also limits the external validity of the results in essential respects, considering that in most real-life situations novel compounds will be encountered in one sort of co(n)textual framing or the other. Moreover, those studies that do take contextual factors into account (Smith et al., 2014; Zlatev et al., 2010; Gagné et al., 2005; Mori & Nagy, 1999) have demonstrated the vast potential of context for overturning any pre-contextually preferred interpretations that might otherwise be explainable in terms of the other factors just mentioned, as well as others, including the existence of an already established whole-word meaning. This observation will be taken further later in the present section and in Section 3.2.1.

3 The original target word was the Danish *Hawaii-pizza* which is a plain noun-noun compound unlike its commonplace English equivalent which is an Adj+N constriction. However, this hardly has much bearing on the point made here. The study in question is addressed in further detail in Section 2.3.1.

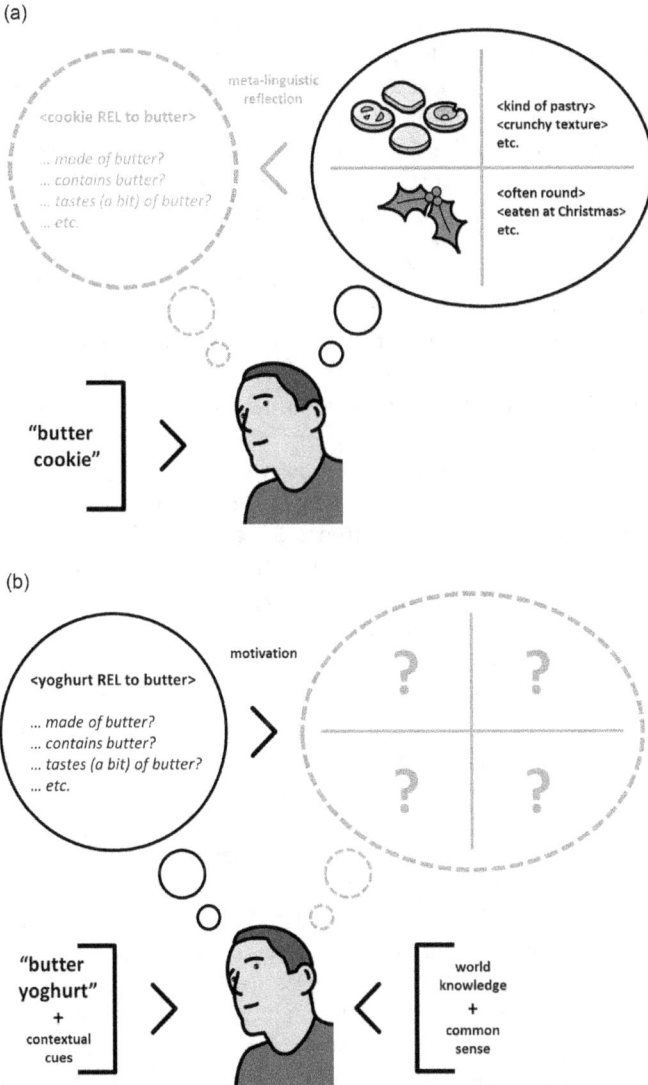

Figure 2.1 Processing of a familiar versus an unfamiliar (novel) noun-noun compound name. (a) Simple decoding of familiar name. If interpreted at all, the noun-noun relation will merely give rise to metalinguistic reflections and expression-based connotations on the part of the recipient. (b) Situated sense-making and concept formation triggered by unfamiliar name. The noun-noun relation is mandatorily interpreted with the recipient's general world knowledge and available contextual cues serving as disambiguating variables.

sentence "as a defence mechanisms against predators, the Alaskan beetle can release a deadly bug spray" (instead of "Debbie made sure that every time she went outside she wore plenty of bug spray"), and by varying the basic design elements brand name, verbal claim, and picture on otherwise identical product packaging fronts, respectively. We will return to the vast potential of multimodal contexts for inducing reframings of the latter sort in Section 3.2.1. At present, the key point is that the surrounding context can make the respondents treat a well-known name *as if* it was new and try to assess its meaning from scratch, using the information at hand (as shown in Figure 2.1b).

What tends to go unnoticed in the mainstream compound-processing literature, however, is that both such reinterpretations and recipients' interpretation of genuinely novel compounds are, in essence, instances of *word acquisition* rather than ordinary language processing. This perspective has mostly been investigated in neighbouring fields, focusing on children's acquisition of words that the rest of us have already acquired (Clark, 2018; Tomasello, 2003; Markman, 1990) and on foreign language learning and teaching (Graves, August, & Mancilla-Martinez, 2013; Prince, 1996) as further addressed in Section 3.1. In both cases, the primary research interest has been recipients' utilization of contextual cues in the widest sense of the term (seeing and touching the denoted objects, hearing parents' or teachers' oral explanations, reading course material, looking at pictures, etc.) for gradually figuring out the meaning of the word, i.e. the Juliet principle. However, when adults encounter genuinely novel or, for that matter, not yet familiar, compounds and other non-arbitrary names, the built-in semantic potential of the name seems to serve as an additional cue (a semantic-to-semantic sign, cf. Wüster, 1959/1960: 191; see also Zlatev et al., 2010: 2811) that *together with* the information deducible from the context will lead the interpretation in a particular direction. That is, the Joyce principle will play its part as well. The final outcome, then, depends on general-purpose heuristics applied to the concrete instance in view also of available general world knowledge and plain common sense, i.e. mechanisms comparable to those further discussed in Section 4.5.3 for Level 4 framings.

Connecting further to the analysis of human categorization presented in Section 1.3.2, this processing will at first only enable the recipient to crystallize some tentative ad hoc concept, but that concept may gradually evolve into a more stable and elaborate one. If the concept is already salient in the relevant population, that will accelerate the process, as argued for *mansplaining* and *deep state* in Section 1.3.2. As still more people encounter the name in Level 3 contexts that support the whole-word meaning in question, an intersubjective consensus will gradually emerge that links the name directly to the concept in question and will be valid to these people even in the most neutral context. Those who share that consensus will therefore no longer need to split up and analyse the name (i.e. resort to the Joyce principle) in order to retrieve the whole-word meaning in question and use the name accordingly. That is, they will reach the equilibrium state shown in Figure 2.1a. What is left is a potential for metalinguistic reflection which may trigger certain expression-based connotations, just at the name may, at any time, be *re*framed by a contradictive Level 3 context, starting the whole process anew (i.e. changing the scenario back to the one shown in Figure 2.1b).

2.4 Lessons Learned from Joyce

What are the practical implications of these empirical findings to professional communicators and to anyone who wants to understand when and how choosing one motivation for a name in preference to another makes a tangible difference?

First, the findings suggest in which situations the Joyce principle should be considered a major strategic factor alongside the Juliet principle and in which not. The former is the case when the declared intention of the communicator is to introduce a genuinely novel name (or profoundly change the meaning of an existing one) rather than merely selecting a well-known name among other alternatives to convey a particular message. Apart from the scenarios already discussed, this also includes the suggestion of substitute names intended to take over (parts of) the meaning of existing ones, as illustrated earlier by *sex worker* versus *prostitute*. By contrast, it is hardly worth anyone's effort to substitute and/or reframe well-established and semantically uncontroversial names such as *cocktail*, *monkey wrench*, or *French fries* despite their arguably less-than-optimal (and/or obsolete) motivations – even if *Freedom fries* was in fact at some point suggested as a substitute for the latter in US English to send a political message (Benczes, 2006a). Brand names such as *Reebok* and *Volkswagen* illustrate the same point.

Second, it becomes clear what can and what can *not* be achieved by creating a name with one motivation in preference to another in those cases where this can in fact make a difference. While the name can never tell the whole story on its own, it can foreground particular components of the (always more complex) conceptual structures it is supposed to lexicalize, say, by presenting smartphones as *smart* and sleep hygiene as a kind of *hygiene*. If poorly chosen, it may, however, also foster an undesired balance between key components of the intended concept as we saw it with the Danish name *betalingsring* (lit. ≈ 'payment ring') earlier; here, a name such as *miljøring* (lit. ≈ 'ecoring') might have become a virtual game changer, or rather a better game initiator since launching alternative names *post-festum* turned out not to be enough to change the negative spiral of events viewed from the Danish government's perspective. Moreover, such influences on the concept's final structure may well prevail even after the name has become conventionalized and the analysis of its motivation therefore becomes optional. That is, the name may still serve as a "reminder" of the rationale behind its original motivation on the level of metalinguistic reflections, though even that effect tends to erode with time.

None of the above alters the strong potential of the Juliet principle which may, indeed, overrule any Joyce-principle influences from the very outset. For example, if a new brand name is backed up by massive and versatile marketing communications (advertising, mass media coverage, word of mouth), it can "say" almost anything literally and still be successful (this perspective is taken further in Section 3.2). But that will, of course, take a greater communicative effort than if the built-in semantic potential of the name plays along.

Another perspective is added to the whole issue when names crystallized in one language are transposed to other languages using word elements and combinations of such that support an unforeseen literal reading. Particularly for commercial names, numerous more or less well-documented examples flourish in the popular, not least in the digital, media, though few of them have been subject to more deep-going analyses (an exception being certain recurrent naming flaws made by foreign companies in China; see Section 1.2). Among the more credible examples from other languages is Mitsubishi's car model *Pajero* which was introduced under that name but hastily renamed *Montero* for Spanish-speaking markets, allegedly because *pajero* is slang for 'masturbator' in several South American Spanish dialects. Another much-quoted example, turning to China once again, is Microsoft's software program *Bing* for which the sound structure of the original name was rendered by means of a logogram character that (also) means 'disease' in

Mandarin Chinese. For further details on these and other examples, see e.g. Language Nerds (2019); Gitlin (2009); Walker (n.d.). The simple point intended here is that not only contextual reframings within the same language (as discussed in Section 2.3), but also a change in general linguistic surroundings seems capable to "re-evoke" the Joyce principle and make recipients interpret a name from scratch.

Speaking of naming more broadly, many attempts have been made to pinpoint what a "good name" is, or should be, within fields that span from marketing and branding (Arora, Kalro, & Sharma, 2015; Di Francesco, 2013; Riezebos et al., 2003: 104–125; Kohli & LaBahn, 1997) to the management and standardization of professional terminologies (Ten Hacken & Panocová, 2015; Wright & Budin, 1997; ISO, 2009: 7.3.1–7.3.8), or the naming of political movements (Shah, 2018). This has fostered a multitude of overlapping and sometimes contradictive criteria (e.g. transparency versus brevity), most of which relate to inherent properties of the name, i.e. to the Joyce principle. The present analysis, then, might contribute to a more balanced approach where not only the built-in semantic potential of the name, but the totality of factors that determine the consolidation of its final meaning in the relevant target group(s) are considered and operated upon in parallel.

Methodologically, this requires a combination of in-depth conceptual analysis with assessments of plausible spontaneous interpretations of candidate names by the target group in view of expectable background knowledge and pre-established cognitive schemas and rationales. The next step is pre-testing, considering also the impact of surrounding contextual cues, as further discussed from Section 3.1 onwards. While more time-consuming, this may prove a useful supplement to the reliance on intuition and accumulated practical experience which remains the major driver (and not per definition a bad one) behind such naming decisions today.

3 Naming & Framing at Level 3
The Juliet Principle

3.1 The Multimodal Character of Level 3 Framings

A major virtue of Collins's Juliet metaphor (and of Shakespeare's original observation) is that it subsumes under a common heading a number of factors that play the same basic role in naming & framing processes but are otherwise rarely viewed in integration. Thus, apart from the built-in motivation that many expression-units have (viz. the Joyce principle as further discussed in the previous chapter), the only factors that can influence how we understand a name, and modify that over time, are how (including when and where) it is used by others and how we experience whatever they use it about. In other words, the genesis of lexical meanings depends on contextual cues in the widest sense of the term (see also Gennari, MacDonald, Postle, & Seidenberg, 2007; Nagy, 1995).[1]

To illustrate, the reader might reflect on how (s)he acquired the meaning of the name *smartphone*. For the author of this book, the full sequence of events would seem to include hearing the word on TV and reading it in printed and online media without taking much notice at first. Moreover, afterwards it is hard to determine if it was *smartphone* or the brand-specific name *iPhone* that was encountered first, since the framings tended to overlap at that time. Subsequent

---

[1] The meaning-in-context issue has come to cover rather different sub-issues in the language-theoretical literature. As for the lexical (word) level, this includes both how context helps choosing between different conventionalized meanings of polysemous words (Williams, 1992) and how different parts of the conventionalized meaning(s) of words are activated differently in different contexts (sometimes referred to as different "senses," e.g. Paradis, 2004). However, our present focus is on the way contextual cues contribute to the of genesis and evolution of such conventionalized meanings in the first place, ensuring their subsequent validity also in neutral contexts such as dictionary entries (see also Zlatev, Smith, van de Weijer, & Skydsgaard, 2010).

cues included hearing friends and colleagues praising their new smartphones, seeing people using the devices, receiving messages, films, and music sent from smartphones (but received by e-mail), seeing ads and reading sales offers concerning smartphones, and ultimately buying one. The latter step added hands-on sensory experience with using a smartphone and gradually learning which features (at that point) were common to most smartphones or model- or brand-specific. Only during the preparation of this book did the process involve consulting explicit definitions and overviews of the topic, adding yet new details. In other words, still more specific candidates for essential and prototypical components involving both sensory and propositional information were added to the emerging concept along the way, and that process continues ... for all of us.

Understanding how such influences combine and interact in shaping the meaning of particular names seems to constitute a reasonable topic for investigation in its own right. For strategically minded communicators, an additional issue is to what degree they can be controlled. Several very different disciplines contribute pieces to that puzzle.

Research into children's acquisition of new words (Clark, 2018; Vygotsky, 2012 [1934]); Goldberg, 2006: 69–102; Tomasello, 2003: 43–93; Piaget, 2002 [1926]; Markman, 1990) addresses the strategies applied by children at different ages for filtering out and generalizing information from the speech of adults and from non-verbal (sensory) cues to make still more qualified guesses about the meanings of still more abstract words. Research into foreign language learning and teaching furthermore considers factors such as classroom instruction, illustrations, and the role of translation, both for children and adults (Graves, August, & Mancilla-Martinez, 2013; Prince, 1996; Willis, 1981). Other facets yet are added by research into adults' spontaneous interpretation of unfamiliar compounds and other non-arbitrary words as already discussed in Section 2.3.

Taking a different perspective, terminology management research and practice stress the importance of explicit and, ideally, normative definitions, though it is also recognized that this ideal is not always met (ISO, 2009: 6.1–6.5; Giboreau et al., 2007; de Bessé, 1997). Pursuing other goals yet, marketing researchers and practitioners have investigated which features can be verbally ascribed (and in fact given) to new types of products in order for them, and their names, to be comprehended and accepted (Gattol, Sääksjärvi, Gill, & Schoormans, 2016; Charette, Hooker, & Stanton, 2015).

Moreover, the construction of brand images is usually based on a vast array of cues surrounding the brand name, spanning from colours, shapes, and images on the product itself to advertising, independent media coverage, sponsorships, celebrity endorsement, storytelling, word of mouth, and so on (Keller, 2016, 2001; Rindell, 2008; Fog, Budtz, & Yakaboylu, 2005; Aaker, 1991). Systematic framing efforts in the public sphere are also vital to what we here label naming & framing at Level 4 with a traditional emphasis on verbal means, but often involving also visual ones such as photos and films. The primary goal here is to influence public opinion on subject matters that go beyond the meaning of single words, yet with a strong potential for also affecting peoples understanding of the words used for this purpose taken individually; see Sections 4.1–4.3.

All such manifestations of the Juliet principle complete the toolbox that communicators can draw on when engaging in goal-driven naming & framing activities. This may not be new to practitioners (Mautner, 2016; Rundh, 2009), but it does not always transpire from the more specialized areas of research mentioned earlier. A framework capable of facilitating a more holistic understanding across such domains is offered by the paradigm known as multimodal communication research (Ledin & Machin, 2020; Powell, Boomgaarden, de Swert, & de Vreese, 2019; Jewitt, Bezemer, & O'Halloran, 2016; Forceville, 2014; Jones, 2014; Holsanova, 2012; Kress, 2010; Kress & van Leeuwen, 2001; see also Section 0.3). The fundamental insight embraced by this research is that most communicative processes involve a combination of different semiotic modalities (spoken and/or written language, pictures, logos, colours, shapes, gesture, immediate sensory-motor experiences, and so on[2]) and that the communicative effects of choosing particular combinations of such modalities in preference to others, considering also recipients' ways and sequences of decoding them, can and should be a research focus in its own right.

Present-day multimodal communication research draws upon and combines insights gained across a number of established disciplines, including visual rhetoric, perceptual and cognitive

---

[2] The exact delimitation of these modalities may vary with the specific purpose of the analysis but overarching distinguishing features include the human senses appealed to, the matter in which the signs materialize, and their degree of conventionalization versus immediate intelligibility; see Forceville (2014: 51–52) for an inclusive approach embracing most such variations.

psychology, cognitive pragmatics, social semiotics, functional linguistics, and conversation analysis (see Jewitt et al., 2016 for a comprehensive overview). Despite variations in theoretical orientation and empirical focus, the overarching agenda could be summarized as follows: First, rather than merely recognizing the existence and co-occurrence of different semiotic modalities, the emphasis is put on establishing what unites and what differentiates their communicative potential taken separately, and which possibilities and constraints different combinations of such modalities offer to communicators when pursuing particular communicative goals. Second, apart from focusing on sheer potential, emphasis is also put on recipients' actual decoding of the total semiotic mix in running communication, in that the order in which its individual elements are attended to (and whether they are attended to at all) may yield very different results.

At the same time, and partially in parallel, an increased interest in understanding the full potential of different combinations of (what we here call) semiotic modalities for pursuing particular communicative goals has developed across a number of more performance-oriented disciplines with a view to practices such as news coverage, advertising, packaging and web design, health promotion, and others. Much of this research does, however, not refer directly to the broader agenda described earlier, though some does (Fenko, Nicolaas, & Galetzka, 2018; Powell, Boomgaarden, de Swert, & de Vreese, 2015; Kim, Thomas, Sankaranarayana, Gedeon, & Yoon, 2015; Ares et al., 2013; Rundh, 2009; Chandon & Wansink, 2007; Clement, 2007; Sojka & Giese, 2006; Riezebos, Kist, & Kootstra, 2003; see also Section 3.2.1).

Applying insights gained in the totality of domains just mentioned to the investigation of naming & framing processes appears to pose a good opportunity for establishing new collaborative links and synergies within and across them.

3.2 An Illustration: High- versus Low-Budget Route Framing of Brand and Product Names

An example of such a multimodal perspective applied specifically to the contextual framing of novel names (though not expressed in these terms) is the low-budget route versus the high-budget route of brand development suggested by Riezebos et al. (2003: 80–103) in continuation of Collins (1977) and related research (Kent & Allen, 1994).

As anticipated in Section 1.1, the conceptual structures conveyed by brand names seem to require a somewhat different analysis than those conveyed by general names. Thus, the core conceptual function of categorization already lies in the fact that something is (being called), e.g., an *Apple*® product or more specifically an *iPhone*®. The brand value lies in the additional expectations and associations that consumers come to connect with products carrying such names (Keller, 2016; Maurya & Mishra, 2012; Murphy, 1992; Aaker, 1991). The latter best qualify as a variety of prototypical components (both propositional and sensory) according to the general analysis of conceptual structure given in Section 1.3.1; see Figure 1.2. Still, the following analyses appear to be applicable to general names as well, including unprotected (generic) product names such as *smartphone* and *e-cigarette* as we shall see below.

The high-budget route presupposes that the brand name is backed up by extensive advertising. Apart from traditional advertising (paid media), the argument also seems to apply to other forms of proactive market communication such as attracting positive mass media coverage (earned media) and consumer-driven support, e.g., in the social media (shared media) in so far as substantial resources are still spent on promotion and PR to generate and shape that coverage (for an overview of the media strategies mentioned and the still more blurring line between them, see Macnamara, Lwin, Adi, & Zerfass, 2016). Such an approach grants the Juliet principle a predominant role from the outset; the Joyce principle may contribute some leads as well, but this remains optional. A clear-cut example is the brand name *Apple* which means what it means to consumers as a result of extensive and widely distributed marketing communication, as further backed up by people's positive first-hand experiences with the company's products, a factor that however also belongs to the Juliet domain. The original meaning of the word *apple* (i.e. its semantic motivation, see Section 2.2), by contrast, may add some freshness and a twist, but it could hardly have done the job alone (for details on the prehistory of the brand name *Apple*, see Wozniak, 2006: 173–174).

The low-budget route, by contrast, presupposes that the brand image is built up without resorting to any large-scale marketing campaigns. In this case, the immediate communicative potential of the brand name becomes a central factor in combination with such cues that may be extracted from the product itself and/or its immediate surroundings such as the product packaging (Simonet, 2016; Klimchuk & Krasovec, 2013; see also LaPlante-Dube, 2017 on similar strategies applied to services presented as "packages"). In such cases, the communication thus relies on channels that are fully controlled by the brand owner and must be paid for in any case, i.e. a variety of owned media to follow the terminology used earlier, whereas any backup from earned and/or shared media is left to self-driven "viral" processes (Berger, 2014) and the use of paid media is minimized or skipped completely. In this scenario, the Juliet principle and the Joyce principle therefore come to interact more closely in a "microcosmos" directly pertaining to a potential decision-making situation.

A clear-cut example of the low-budget approach is the brand name *Cavi-Art* owned by a company that has built up a worldwide business producing caviar substitutes based on seaweed and aromatic additives.[3] Taking the low-budget-route thinking almost to the limit, the company's sales promotion has from the outset been restricted to simply presenting the products to sales agents, retailers, and ultimately consumers worldwide, without much additional marketing apparently being needed. The motivation (in this case morphological) that can be deduced from the brand name itself seems to have been sufficient for intriguing the viewer in the relevant way, and the rest of the story is told by the familiar shape of the jars and the relatively transparent (even if seemingly contradictory[4]) motivation of the immediate product name *Seaweed Caviar* (with extensions for different variants, e.g. *Black, Red, Wasabi*), likewise placed on the packaging front. No additional verbal or visual cues appear to be required in this case.

3.2.1 Consuming the "Semiotic Cocktail"

The examples illustrate two additional points to be further considered in this and the following sub-section, respectively. The first point is that there will always be a reciprocal influence between all the cues involved in Level 3 framing processes, i.e. they will

---

[3] Jens Møller Products ApS. URL: https://tang-huset.dk/en/tang-huseten/ (accessed June 2020).
[4] The apparent conceptual clash between *seaweed* and *caviar* thus provides an effective trigger for the conceptual restructuring needed to grasp the very essence of the new product and generate a tentative ad-hoc concept that may gradually be further consolidated. One framework suited for a more detailed analysis of the cognitive processes required is conceptual blending theory (Schmid, 2011; Fauconnier & Turner, 2003).

contribute to framing each other. Thus, most of the *Apple*-related framings suggested in Figure 3.1a will also involve other, thematically connected names such as the product-line specific brand names *iPhone, iPad, Apple Watch*, and *MacBook*, and the generic names *smartphone tablet, smartwatch*, and *laptop*. These names all contribute to understanding what *Apple* stands for as a brand name while at the same time qualifying the meaning of each other and, for some, being qualified by the name *Apple*. Non-verbal cues are also part of the overall picture. Thus, the Apple product shown in Figure 3.1a does not carry the name *Apple* at all, only a stylized image of an apple. The link is established through the total multimodal communication surrounding the brand. Likewise, the brand

Figure 3.1 The high-budget route and the low-budget route of brand name framing. (a) Example of the high-budget route: *Apple*®. (b) Example of the low-budget route: *Cavi-Art*®.

name *Cavi-Art* and the immediate (but still manufacturer-specific and legally protected) product name *Seaweed Caviar* mutually contribute to the disambiguating each other in interplay with surrounding visual cues such as the shape of the jar and the images of seaweed and of the product itself on the label (Figure 3.1b).

The process of decoding such multimodal stimuli has become the subject of a still growing body of observational and experimental research, both with and without direct reference to multimodality as a distinct phenomenon (see also Section 3.1). This includes the use of eye-tracking technology for monitoring viewers' distribution of their top-down and bottom-up visual attention (i.e. looking for something and having one's eyes caught by something, respectively, cf. Orquin & Loose, 2013; Chun & Wolfe, 2008) while examining condensed "semiotic cocktails" such as product packaging fronts, IT user interfaces, and news media pages under varying conditions (Fenko et al., 2018; Bulling, 2016; Rebollar, Lidón, Martín, & Puebla, 2015; Ares et al., 2013; Clement, 2007; Holsanova, Rahm, & Holmqvist, 2006; Pieters & Warlop, 1999). It has, for instance, been demonstrated that people tend to seek more information in the surrounding context not only when encountering an unfamiliar product and/or product name, but also when a familiar product name is encountered on a product packaging the total verbal and visual potential of which contradicts the expectable product identity, leading to additional processing time and changed search patterns (Smith, Barratt, & Zlatev, 2014; Ares et al., 2013).

The implications of such observations for understanding the acquisition of novel names were already touched upon in Section 2.3. To illustrate further, let us take a closer look at the former study which targeted Danish compound food names with the aim of assessing to what degree 'X origins physically in Y' can be considered a default reading for noun-noun compounds of the type 'Y [Place Name] +X [Food Name].' This is routinely assumed by consumer organizations and widely (though not unconditionally) backed up by authorities and courts, but sometimes challenged by food companies in public disputes on potentially misleading food naming and labelling (Smith et al., 2014; Smith, Clement, Møgelvang-Hansen, & Selsøe Sørensen, 2011; see also MacMaoláin, 2015, 2007).

It was hypothesized that an interpretation in terms of physical origin was indeed a plausible default reading for novel food names of this type if presented in a neutral context (explainable in terms of conceptual compatibility and analogy, see also Section 2.3). A possible exception would be such cases where consumers' expectable background knowledge of the place and food in question would speak against such an interpretation. This found support in a first experiment in which geographically plausible (yet fictitious) compounds such as *Limfjors-torsk* ('Limfjord cod') and *Loire-brie* ('Loire brie') received mean ratings approaching maximum, whereas potentially contradictive examples such as *Sahara-sild* ('Sahara herring') and *Amazonas-kylling* ('Amazon(-rainforest) chicken') received mean ratings approaching minimum in response to the question "does the place name refer to the physical origin of the product (where the product in itself comes from)?" on a five-point Likert-type scale.

However, in actual life, consumers usually encounter novel commercial food products and their names in/on packages which also carry other verbal and visual cues (whether or not further backed up by more widely distributed consumer-oriented communication, the minimal solution being the low-budget-route scenario shown in Figure 3.1b). To learn more about the decoding of both novel and established Place-Food compounds in such more realistic surroundings, a second experiment was conducted in which Place-Food compounds of both sorts were presented to participants in a similar setup, but placed on stylized packaging fronts either supporting or contradicting the pre-contextually preferred interpretations (which for the established compounds was set equal to the interpretation naturally following from their conventionalized whole-word meaning as established in an informal e-mail inquiry among colleagues). Congruent and incongruent name-context pairings were distributed evenly in a between-groups design. The contextual framings were created by systematically varying the key design elements brand name, verbal claim, and picture on otherwise identical packaging fronts while taking care not to address the made-in issue directly but merely opening alternative paths of interpretation (for further details, see Smith et al., 2014: 122–124).

Figure 3.2a and 3.2b show the contextual framings used for supporting and contradicting the pre-contextually preferred reading of the novel (fictitious) compound name *Amazonas-kylling* ('Amazon (rainforest) chicken') which in this case was one of non-origin (if encountered in a Danish supermarket which was the scenario that the participants were instructed to imagine).

The results showed that not only were such contexts capable of significantly decreasing/increasing the pre-contextually established preferences for/against a physical-origin reading for novel

Naming & Framing at Level 3   49

Figure 3.2 Novel Place-Food compound on schematized packaging fronts (a) supporting and (b) contradicting the pre-contextually preferred interpretation. In the supporting context, the Danish verbal claim reads 'this is what we call free range!' while the brand name is conceived in English, suggesting a global (and environmental) orientation and eliminating the need for translation here. In the contradicting context, the verbal claim reads 'with chili, kidney beans, and cilantro' and the brand name reads something similar to 'Easy Saturday.'

(fictitious) compounds; the same was true for established compounds such as *Hawaii-pizza* ('Hawaiian pizza') which is otherwise hardly ever taken to indicate physical origin in a Danish context and *Samsø-kartofler* ('Samsø potatoes') which is widely known as a name for high-quality fresh potatoes actually grown on the island of Samsø (but which was here alternatively framed as potentially referring to a pre-prepared potato dish that could be produced anywhere).

An important implication for real-life food naming and labelling practices is that the fairness or potential misleadingness of concrete naming and labelling solutions can only be realistically assessed if the total packaging design is taken into account while also considering consumers' real-time decoding of it. That is, such assessments must go substantially beyond what Jones (2014) labels a "language-centric" view of these issues which tends to dominate the administrative and legal practices of most countries today (see also Smith, Møgelvang-Hansen, & Hyldig, 2010).

Furthermore, comparing the rating scores with response times and registrations of eye movements by means of eye-tracking equipment contributed important leads about the underlying decoding processes. To mention just a few informative observations: Overall, participants spent more time looking at the target compounds when presented in incongruent context than when presented in congruent ones. However, across all conditions, the mean response latencies were significantly higher than those registered in the first experiment, indicating that most participants did spent some extra time looking at the surrounding context, even if that this was not strictly required for the familiar compounds for which a response could, in principle, be given by simply fixating the compound and retrieving its well-known whole-word meaning. This can be explained by the capability of the surrounding design elements, particularly the large-scale photos, to attract bottom-up (stimulus-driven) attention automatically by virtue of inherently salient visual features relating to size, colour contrast, presence of human action, and others (cf. Orquin & Loose, 2013; Chun & Wolfe, 2008). The picture was fixated first in the majority of trials and 83.6% looked at least two other elements apart from the target name, thereby adding new potential candidates for situational sense-making and disambiguation (relying, for instance, on cognitive mechanisms comparable to those further discussed in Section 4.5.3 relative to Level 4 framings).

The fact that relatively moderate extra time was nevertheless spent on compounds presented in congruent contexts (with the lowest latencies being observed for familiar compounds presented in such contexts) may, in turn, be plausibly explained by the limited cognitive effort needed to make sense of the respective elements if so desired. By contrast, the incongruent contexts had been deliberately designed to contradict the pre-contextually most plausible interpretation which means that – once they had attracted the viewer's attention – they were likely to induce a shift from bottom-up (stimulus-driven) to top-down (goal-driven) attention, i.e. an active search for a plausible explanation leading to more fixations and re-fixations and more than one "trip round." This is consistent with the significantly higher response latencies registered for both familiar and novel compounds in these conditions and various trends observed in the eye-tracking data. For example, relatively more time was spent on the visually less prominent but potentially more informative verbal claims and relatively less time on the pictures.

While a full understanding of the decoding processes unfolding in settings such as the present still lies far ahead, modelling them experimentally nevertheless adds certain new leads to our current understanding of what is actually going on. A possible direction for continued research would be to apply comparable methods to people's real-time decoding of temporally and visually more remote framings, say, as encountered when surfing the internet for additional information during online shopping or comparing party programs in electoral campaigns. In other words, by encompassing interactive options (see also Ooms et al., 2015), the focus might be extended from individual communicative products to thematically connected products offering different "packages" of multimodal resources to people during transmedial information search, thus complementing existing research on such processes with a new type of data (O'Halloran, Tan, & Marissa, 2017; Kim et al., 2015; Castelló, Morsing, & Schultz, 2013; Giovagnoli, 2011; Darley, Blankson, & Luethge, 2010).

3.2.2 *Control versus Credibility and Effect*

The other additional point illustrated by the examples in Figure 3.1a and b is the varying degree of control that interested stakeholders have over the verbal and visual framing of names that are important to them, and hence over the meanings that people will eventually connect with the names. Brand and product naming is one area where such a control is badly desired by those creating the names, but not always possible. Another clear example of this (while fundamentally different in other respects) is professional terminology, but let us start out by considering the brand and product names discussed in connection with Figure 3.1a and b and extend the focus to other areas of naming & framing in Section 3.3.

As indicated earlier, the value of a brand name lies not so much in owning it legally as in the expectations and associations that consumers come to connect with it (see also Maurya & Mishra, 2012; Rindell, 2008). Both paid and owned media offer brand owners a high degree of control in that respect (at varying levels of cost, as discussed earlier), while earned and shared media may substantially increase credibility, but also involve a higher risk of negative coverage fostering undesired expectations.

For example, when the web medium The Verge at some point echoed Apple's own appraisals of their new generation of ARM processors for iPhones and iPads, stating that "Apple says it is the most powerful chip in a smartphone ever," this is likely to have contributed new positive expectations to the continued conceptual developments around the brand name *Apple*. However, when the very same medium later approached the issue from a more critical angle, less positive elements may have been added as well, yet equally powerful due to the medium's relatively independent status (cf. Hollister's, 2020, overview of contrasting judgements and data). The same applies, say, to independent product reviews in YouTube videos and debates in internet blogs (see also Smith, Fischer, & Yongjian, 2012; Susarla, Oh, & Tan, 2012). Brand owners thus face the dilemma of either trusting their products or services to speak for themselves or engaging in extensive PR and media work, including the establishment of win-win alliances with (otherwise) independent actors (Granata, Tartagilone, & Theodosios, 2019; Cui, Lui, & Guo, 2012). While Cavi-Art consistently relies on the former strategy, Apple subtly combines both.

In addition, there are cases where protected brand status is not even sufficient to restrict the referential use of a name in everyday speech, let alone any additional expectations. Classic examples are *xerox* and *jacuzzi* which have "grown generic" in many varieties of English despite their (still valid) status as registered brand names (see Harrell, 2014 for a continued list). Conversely, many consumers worldwide still conceive *feta* as a generic name for a particular type of (Greek-style) cheese regardless that the name became a protected designation of origin (PDO) restricted to Greek products in 2002 (cf. MacMaoláin, 2007: 108–119).

In the case of entirely unprotected (generic) product names such as *smartphone* and *vegan caviar* (if not *Seaweed Caviar* which enjoys a certain protection as a registered trademark), the array of possible framings comes even further beyond the control of individual stakeholders. Yet, such framings may still interfere with their collective interests. For example, public concerns that *smartphones* may seriously damage children's physical and mental health (NCI, 2019; Glatter, 2014) hardly contribute to the positive brand image or sales figures of any manufacturer of such devices, be it Apple, Samsung, or Huawei. Related examples are the diverse and sometimes conflicting public framings of names such as *e-cigarettes* or *CO_2 emissions* where commercial interests collide with societal concerns about health protection and climate change (Yates et al., 2015; Avineri & Waygood, 2013). Importantly, the mapping of such conflicting public framings would seem to indicate that they do not only influence people's general expectations to the referents, but also their conceptualization of them in terms of number of and balance between (what we here call) prototypical and essential conceptual components (see Section 1.3.1 and Figure 1.2). For example, to some people e-cigarettes are first and foremost a kind of stimulant that poses a serious threat to public health, while to others they are an efficient aid for quitting tobacco smoking. Both positions find some support in the research literature as echoed in the wider public debate (Alexander, 2017; Shahab et al., 2017; Yu et al., 2016; Yates et al., 2015).

In turn, becoming aware of such conflicting framings may lead some recipients to experience the so-called cognitive dissonance, i.e. emotional and physical discomfort caused by exposure to contradictive information, ideas, and beliefs, a well-documented psychological response to which is to avoid or neglect framings that are inconsistent with whatever "truth" one has decided to go with (O'Keefe, 2016: 76–97; Festinger, 1957). In today's information-intensive societies, the ultimate consequence is the formation of what has been labelled (information or filter) bubbles, a term already mentioned in Section 2.2 as an example of non-arbitrary naming, i.e. a psychological state characterized by extreme selectivity with regard to what information, and hence which framings, a person will allow him- or herself to be exposed to (cf. Nguyen, Hui, Harper, Terveen, & Konstan, 2014; Resnick, Garrett, Kriplean, Munson, & Stroud, 2013; Pariser, 2011). We will return to the ethical implications of these developments in Sections 4.4–4.6.

3.3 Names Negotiated

Taking the discussion beyond the commercial sphere, the examples just discussed also illustrate the more general circumstance that people often display different, yet related, understandings of what a given name means. According to the present framework, such differences can be seen as caused by the co-existence of conflicting contextual framings of the name at Level 3. While the decisive role of competing framings in people's comprehension of more complex subject matters has long been a major concern in the study of naming & framing processes at (what we here call) Level 4, as further addressed in Chapter 4, the implications for describing the meaning of individual names have been less systematically considered. The issue is largely neglected in mainstream linguistic theorizing as marginal exceptions to the dominant conception of language(s) as intersubjectively agreed code(s). However, the frequency of such "exceptions" has from time to time attracted the interest of other scholars, in particular philosophers (Devitt & Sterelny, 1999; Pessin & Goldberg, 1996; Putnam, 1975a,b; Gallie, 1955).

Gallie (1955) thus speaks of *essentially contested concepts* conveyed by names such as *democracy, fairness*, and *human rights* (see also Bovaird, 2004; Hobson, Lewis, & Siim, 2002; Garre, 1999). It is in the very nature of such concepts to be constantly challenged and (re)negotiated regarding both the exact number and mutual importance of (what we here call) essential and prototypical components (see Figure 2.1) and their applicability to real-life circumstances such as the state of democracy in Turkey or the fairness of EU immigration policies. Related analyses also seem to apply to other types of professionally negotiable vocabulary such as the business term (and buzzword) *startup* already discussed in Section 2.2. Different authors and practitioners tend to foreground different attributes among those listed in Section 2.2 (and others) as the most important preconditions for a company to be a genuine startup (Marius, 2016; Blank & Dorf, 2012; Graham, 2004). And yet, the pivotal role of the term itself remains the same throughout these discussions. Another example would be the diverse framings of the term *framing* in language and communication research (see e.g. Entman, 1993, and this book).

Speaking of naming more generally, Putnam (1975a; see also 1975b) suggests a hypothesis of "division of linguistic labour"[5]

---

[5] Putnam presents his hypothesis as part of a larger argument in defence of the much-debated philosophical position that the reference of a name can be dealt with independently of "intangible" psychological variables such as concepts and thoughts. However, as demonstrated also by e.g. Keil, Stein, Webb, Billings, & Rozenblit (2008), Geeraerts, (2006), and Lakoff (1987), the argument as such is not inconsistent with a cognitivist position which accepts the human

according to which people collaborate on knowing (different fragments of) the meaning of the words they use. It is assumed that ordinary language users connect many words only with vague and incomplete concepts (or "stereotypes") which are however sufficient for ensuring successful communication in a great many instances. Whenever in doubt, they will however leave the final judgement to those members of society who have been granted the status of "experts" of the domain in question. For example, most people who use the word *gold* are not able to determine if something is really gold or not. Yet if an expert tells somebody that whatever (s)he has been referring to as gold is actually something else, the person will (hopefully) stop using that name. Likewise, many of us know that a *wombat* is some kind of animal that lives in Australia and that *foie gras* is a celebrated French culinary speciality, but would still leave it to an expert to decide if the name applies in concrete instances.

One among several potential objections to Putnam's argument (see also e.g. Geeraerts, 2006; Pessin & Goldberg, 1996) is that it does not distinguish between "division of linguistic labour" and plain polysemy, i.e. the fact that some words can have different but related meanings, including specialized meaning(s) in professional language (see also Sager, 1990). For example, most speakers of English distinguish *trees* from *plants*, and in this case a biologist' claim that a tree is actually a type of plant will hardly affect the use of these names in everyday speech. Another complication is that experts may also disagree among themselves (as we saw it earlier with e-cigarettes and startups) and that different categories of experts may resort to different types of criteria for determining the exact reference of the same name, yielding different results. Thus, to a chemist (at work), *gold* is first and foremost an element (Au) with specific chemical properties, whereas to a jeweller (at work) it is mostly a category of alloys containing Au but also other metals used for making jewellery. It is thus not necessarily given in advance which experts will be the most relevant to consult in which situations, or whether individual language users will consult any experts at all.

---

mind (and, for some, the brain) as valid and methodologically accessible objects of scientific inquiry. From such a position, Putnam's observations provide an excellent framework for addressing certain evident gaps in the analysis of lexical meanings as intersubjectively valid entities that have largely been neglected in mainstream language theory but noted by others (see also e.g. Gee, 2015: 24–29 for a social-linguistically founded argument going in the same direction).

None of this alters the basic observation that, in some cases, different framings of a name at Level 3 will not result in classic polysemy, but in a state of asymmetric interdependence between the meanings connected with the name by different individuals. Transposed to rhetoric terms (McCroskey, 2016: 82–107; Carey, 1994), the authority (ethos) of some language users may influence the propositional content (logos) and emotional load (pathos) that other people come to convey and disseminate further by using the name, yet without being able to formulate the underlying criteria or foreseeing the total range of implication themselves (as to the emotional dimension, see also Lecheler, Bos, & Vliegenthart, 2015).

A way of encompassing this circumstance into the analysis of conceptual structure given in Section 1.3.1 (see Figure 1.2) would be to describe ordinary language users' "versions" of the concepts in question as containing a number of empty slots for which only experts can provide the relevant fillers (to state it in slot/filler terms, e.g. Busse, 2017; Ran & Duimering, 2010; Gagné & Spalding, 2006). In the case of *smartphone* analysed in Figure 1.2 in Section 1.3.1, for example, most users of the name are hardly aware that such devices must contain a CPU (central processing unit) and AD and DA converters in order to operate, even though they are likely to expect that there must be some kind of advanced electronic circuits inside that make the thing work. However, to people who have that additional knowledge, it will not only be part of, but count as essential components in their "version" of the concept in question. The latter circumstance is indicated by the grey-toned elements in Figure 1.2.

Likewise, many people are aware that genuine *foie gras* has to meet some kind of criteria in terms of taste, texture, origin, method of preparation, etc. (corresponding to empty conceptual slots which in this case relate to both sensory and propositional information), but specifying the adequate fillers is, again, left to trusted experts. Furthermore, in a case like *gold* even the basic nature of the additional information required to fill the (presumable) slots may remain fuzzy to many language users so that the division of linguistic labour ultimately comes down to a conceptual component that could be described as <category membership must be confirmed by a societally authorized expert>.

In cases such as *smartphone*, *foie gras*, and *gold*, the sensitivity to experts' final judgements is likely to come down to factors such as expectations to functionality and to social prestige and price. However, it is less intuitively clear if Putnam's predictions would also hold, say, for *hotdog, hipster,* or *fake news* where the body of potential "experts" is more heterogeneous and people might ultimately prefer to rely on their own judgements. What is clearly needed here is harder empirical evidence on the degree to which competing framings of a name may interfere with each other even on the level of one and the same individual's understanding and use of that name under varying conditions.

A first step in that direction was taken in an in-depth quantitative and qualitative review of 821 Danish legal disputes on allegedly misleading food naming and labelling (Møgelvang-Hansen, 2010; Smith et al., 2009). The review showed that ordinary consumers, culinary experts, NGO activists, food manufacturers, and government officials resort to very different criteria and sources of information when judging whether a concrete product lives up to the name under which it is sold and qualifies, say, as real *mead, macaroons, surimi shrimps,* or a *smoothie* (none of the categories mentioned being covered by legally enforceable food standards). In a follow-up experimental study (Smith et al., 2013) it was demonstrated that pre-exposure to authoritative definitions (as compared to a taste-samples-only and a taste-samples-plus-written-product-facts condition) significantly affected consumers' typicality judgements of alternative taste samples for a traditional Danish bakery product such as *makroner* ($\approx$ 'macaroons'), but had no significant effect in the case of *smoothies* where consumers seemed to rely on their own (no less critical) judgements.

Such results lend partial empirical support to Putnam's hypothesis, taking the issue beyond decades of philosophical hair-splitting, while also offering some indications of its scope and limitations. Related test setups might prove applicable to other communicative domains involving a wider range of contextual framings, say, to assess the degree to which professional stakeholders' contributions to the public debate affect ordinary citizens' understanding and use of terms such as *sustainable consumption, climate justice,* or *cybersecurity* under varying conditions. That is: Can the concepts that individual people connect with such terms be described as cognitively consistent at least for each single individual at a given moment in time (while still varying between individuals and open to external influence and gradual evolution), or might a more realistic description be to see them as fractioned samples of potentially self-contradictory (dissonant) conceptual content even in the mind of the single individual?

3.4 Is the Name Wrong or Is the World Going Wrong?

A final implication of the existence of competing framings at Level 3 is their role in the emergence of what was referred to as substitute names in Section 2.2, i.e. in deliberate attempts to re-name things that have a name already. The demand for such names is often presented in the Joyce-principle vein, i.e. as a desire to find a name that "says" something better (or worse, if negative framing is the purpose) than known alternatives, e.g. *sex worker* (which offers more explicit support for claiming societal legitimacy than *prostitute*) or *information war* (which sounds more disturbing than *strategic communications*); see Section 2.2 for further details.

However, in some cases, the need for a new name rather seems to be rooted in previous framings of the existing alternative(s) at Level 3, i.e. in the Juliet principle. For example, both *African American* and *black American* are relatively broadly accepted as demographic designations in modern US English (for possible reasons for preferring one or the other, see Harris, 2014; Agyemang, Bhopa, & Bruijnzeels, 2005), whereas *negro* is nowadays ethically and politically entirely unacceptable. Yet, this hardly comes down to the original motivations of the respective names, considering that *negro* means 'black' in Spanish. The situation is however amply explained by the offensive and inhumane utterances and actions that have accompanied the latter name earlier in the US history (and, alas, sometimes do even today); see Painter (2006) for a historical account. Likewise, earlier layers of framings may explain why *persuasion* is now preferred to the (once quite uncontroversial) name *propaganda* when speaking, say, of health promotion or election campaigns, notwithstanding that *propaganda* literally means 'to spread or propagate something' which, arguably, sounds less manipulative than *persuading* one's audience (for further discussion on the societal evaluations and history of these terms, see Jowett & O'Donnell, 2018). In short, what may ultimately need change are some people's conceptualizations of and attitudes towards whatever a name denotes, not the name as such. In that respect, substituting the name can only play an auxiliary (but still important) part, while any final settlement of the matter depends on framings at Level 3 which are determined by broader developments in society at large.

4 Naming & Framing at Level 4

The Lexical Toolbox of Issues Management and Its Multimodal Surroundings

4.1 Beyond the Meaning of Individual Names

Examples like those considered in Section 3.4 lead us further to naming & framing at Level 4. When it comes to more complex subject matters such as the societal status and rights of ethnic groups or moral and political limits to public campaigning, the contextual framings of interest not only shape our understanding of individual names (though essential parts of such framings may be encapsulated in a single name as we have just seen; this point is taken further in Section 4.3) but also affect the way we determine what is good or bad, right or wrong, relevant or irrelevant, an asset or a threat, and so on, relative to a wider subject taken as a whole and to various more specific issues within it.[1]

In both respects, the effect is achieved through the communicator's choice of (other) words that lead recipients' thoughts and emotions in particular directions, as further supported by non-verbal cues such as photos and graphics and/or immediate sensory contact with whatever is referred to, as discussed in Chapter 3 for single names. Such multimodal framings thus (also) play a vital role when a broader subject and its sub-issues are identified and assessed, that is, as a tool for *issues management* in a broad sense of the term (for a more specific usage in PR, see Section 4.2).

The totality of semiotic resources used for communicating about a given subject are also referred to as a discourse in some research traditions, yet with some variation in definition,

---

1 As we shall soon see, the sub-issues of interest may ultimately be as specific as the nutritional value of a particular food product and the Level 4 framing come down to the choice of a single word or word-picture combination. However, from the perspective taken in this chapter, the question is not what the word means or what the picture depicts as such, but how choosing them in preference to other options in a particular communicative context for conveying a particular message may affect recipients' beliefs and feelings about the sub-issue in question.

methodological approaches, and research foci (Jones, 2017; Mautner, 2016; Fairclough, 2013; Widdowson, 1995; Tannen, 1993); other influential frameworks, however, approach otherwise closely related matters in different terms (e.g. Entman, 1993; Goffman, 1974). To maintain the cross-disciplinary dialogue aimed at from the outset, we will therefore abstain from simply equating the study of naming & framing at Level 4 to discourse analysis (though, in many respects, it is), considering also that the points that need to be made may equally well be accommodated by choosing the appropriate one among more particular terms such as issues, contexts, domains, and modalities.

To take yet an example of conflicting framings, focusing now at Level 4 and on global politics rather than on product naming and branding: If a news medium (say, Fox News) quotes the US authorities for having *proof* that the Syrian *regime* has carried out a *chemical weapon attack* against *civilians* accompanied by pictures of children receiving urgent medical treatment, this tells one story. If another news medium (say, Russia Today) quotes Russian authorities for having *proof* that an *alleged* chemical attack was *staged* and filmed in Syria by *collaborators* of foreign *intelligence services* to *discredit* the Syrian *government*, accompanied by a photo of a seemingly unharmed boy who was (allegedly) among the victims shown in the film, this tells a different story. Some news reports have attempted to cover both angels while displaying a varying degree of confidence in the sources available (Wintour, MacAskill, Borger, & Chrisafis, 2018; BBC News, 2018). In this respect, the example also illustrates the complicated interplay between the original outlets of such framings (here: governments) and their dissemination in earned, shared, paid, and owned media, as discussed at some length in 3.2ff for commercial messages (for more examples and evidence pertaining to global politics, see Hammond, 2018; Ojala, Pantti, & Kangas, 2017; Powell, 2017; Pollack, 2004).

4.2 A Fractured Paradigm: Entman and Later Developments

"Framing" in the present sense, with or without the addition of "naming," is probably the most extensively addressed phenomenon among those investigated under that heading in the research literature up till now. A wide variety of partially overlapping theoretical paradigms have contributed to the topic. These span from overarching philosophical agendas, in particular that of social constructivism (Scheufele, 1999; Brown, 1995) which also entails the fundamental question of whether an "objective" reality beyond our framings of it exists at all (a discussion which is however beyond the scope of the present work), through various directions of sociology (Vliegenthar & van Zoonen, 2011; Goffman, 1974), cognitive and social psychology (Fiske & Taylor, 2013; Nelson, Oxley, & Clawson, 1997; Loftus & Palmer, 1974), linguistically and sociologically oriented discourse analysis (Jones, 2017; Mautner, 2016; Fairclough, 2013; Tannen, 1993), and cognitive linguistics and pragmatics (Fauconnier & Tuner, 2003; Verschueren, 1998) to rhetoric (Lynch & Zoller, 2015) and anthropology (Hoeyer, 2005). During the latest years, a shift has furthermore taken place from mostly seeing (what we here call) Level 4 framings as an essentially language-driven endeavour to also considering the effect of combining different semiotic modalities into multimodal wholes (Powell, Boomgaarden, de Swert, & de Vreese, 2019; Forceville, 2014; Jones, 2014).

The diversity is equally rich when it comes to methodological approaches and combinations of such (Elish & Boyd, 2018; O'Halloran, Tan, Pham, Bateman, & Vande Moere, 2018; Bail, 2014; Bruni, Tran, & Baroni, 2014) and to areas of practical application (as reviewed in Section 0.1). Notably, the latter include issues management in a more specific PR-strategic sense, referring to companies' and other actors' ongoing monitoring of and, if need be, proactive intervention with public framings that may potentially interfere with their strategic interests (Heath & Palenchar, 2008; Crable & Vibbert, 1985). A partially related, while often more negatively loaded, conception is that of spin or spin doctoring (Miller & Dinan, 2008; Esser, Reinemann, & Fan, 2000).

In sum, the picture is rather heterogenous. However, in an influential early study, Entman (1993) argues that instead of seeing the (already then) fractured nature of framing research as a drawback, this ostensive weakness could be turned into a strength by identifying and more clearly defining the common core that evidently runs through most existing treatments of the subject. This renders contributions from a variety of complementary disciplines both welcome and necessary. Pursuing this goal, Entman suggests that to frame is to *"select some aspects of a perceived reality and make them more salient in a communicating text, in such a way as to promote a particular problem definition, causal interpretation, moral evaluation, and/or treatment recommendation"* (Entman, 1993: 52; author's original italics).[2] It might be added that even if the emphasis in the

---

2 Entman thus applies the term *salient* in a somewhat broader sense than the one adopted in Section 1.3.2, namely for referring to the perceived importance and/ or prominence of particular aspects of a given wider subject matter, whereas in

passage quoted is on "text" and hence words, in subsequent work, Entman stresses the potential contribution of non-verbal (visual) framings to the final outcome (Entman, 2003; 2004), thus taking a multimodal perspective concordant with that adopted in the present work (see also e.g. Powell et al., 2019; Meijers, Remmelswaal, & Wonneberger, 2018).

Despite all later developments, Entman's (1993) definition remains widely acknowledged and cited as an operational point of departure for continued investigation of (what we here call) naming & framing at Level 4 (16.714 citations registered in Google Scholar so far[3]). What has followed is a continued diversification and refinement of concrete framing techniques (agenda setting, use of selective comparisons, re- and counter-framings, storytelling, strategic use of metaphors, and so on) and extensions of such techniques to still new fields. Both aspects are amply covered in the existing literature on (what we call) naming & framing at Level 4 as summarized in Section 0.1 and above. What the present work might add, then, is some further elaboration on two essential topics which are also raised by Entman (1993) yet with no claim of an exhaustive treatment.

The first topic is how naming & framing processes on (what we here call) Level 4 connect to (what we here call) naming & framing processes at Levels 1 and 3, as mediated by Level 2. The second topic is the ethical implications that emerge from the still more extensive and professionalized use of framing techniques in public space. We will consider these topics in turn.

4.3 Understanding the Full Ecosystem of Naming & Framing

Elaborating on an observation by Gamson (1992), Entman notes that "a frame can exert great social power *when embedded in a term* [...]" and continues:

> Once a term is widely accepted, to use another is to risk that target audiences will perceive the communicator as lacking

---

Section 1.3.2 (and below) it refers to comparable qualities of concepts for categories of individual entities which bring them "first in line" for being provided with a single name. Both points are essential to the present discussion and the respective uses of the term are not mutually exclusive, but deserve brief mention for clarity.

3 URL: https://scholar.google.dk/scholar?hl=da&as_sdt=0%2C5&q=entman+1993&btnG (accessed June 2020).

credibility – or will even fail to understand what the communicator is talking about. Thus the power of a frame can be *as great as that of language itself*

(1993: 55; my italics, VS)

This observation elegantly summarizes the key argument pursued throughout the preceding chapters of this book regarding naming & framing at Levels 1–3 with implications also for Level 4.

As already argued, tentative conceptualizations of whatever is ultimately provided with a name are likely to have a salient status in the minds of some people even before a name is suggested (following Barsalou's dynamic understanding of human categorization as presented in Section 1.3.2); yet, the cognitive and communicative impact of the content ultimately lexicalized can be substantially increased by the very fact of it being enrolled into something as seemingly objective and indisputable as human language (see also the discussion of linguistic relativism in Section 1.2). All four levels of naming & framing both contribute to and are affected by these processes.

To revisit a case considered earlier: What is known as *sleep hygiene* today would hardly have become a distinct medical field without "having a name for it" (at Level 1); yet, that name has likewise contributed to shaping the scientific and public understanding of the wider subject of sleeping disorders, as supported also by other keywords such as *sleep cycle, bedtime routines, powernap, sleep apnea,* and *CPAP treatment* accompanied by visual and other immediate sensory cues (lending themselves to analysis at Level 4). In turn, the meanings of each of these names – and of *sleeping disorders* and *sleep hygiene*, for that matter when taken as names of the overall subjects – have been shaped by the verbal and non-verbal contextual cues surrounding them in ongoing communication (shifting the focus back to Level 3). Moreover, in some cases, conflicting framings may lead different people to understand the same names in somewhat different ways (requiring further analysis at Level 3, but with potential implications also for Level 4). For example, experts disagree on the exact period of time required for a short sleep to be a physiologically beneficial *powernap* and this may have important implications also for peoples' comprehension of sleeping strategies in other respects. In all that, the built-in motivation of the names involved (Level 2) may either support the understanding intended by the initial communicators, as *sleep hygiene* seems to have succeeded to do in the present example, or obscure it as when the Danish government launched a new initiative under the name *betalingsring* (lit. ≈ 'payment ring') where e.g. *miljøring* (lit. ≈ 'ecoring') might have done a better job; see Section 2.2.

A perhaps more broadly comprehensible example which has furthermore been subject to extensive investigation from a declared framing perspective is *climate change* (Poberezhskaya & Ashe, 2018; Drews & van den Bergh, 2016; O'Brien, Eriksen, Nygaard, & Schjolden, 2007). Despite the seemingly transparent and unbiased morphological motivation of that name, what it denotes (and ultimately "really means") has been framed and counter-framed by interested actors as everything from a here-and-now threat to life in Earth to ideologically motivated fiction (for an overview of some extremes flourishing in the current debates, see Grist, 2020). In turn, these framings also involve other names such as *global warming, greenhouse gasses, CO_2 footprint, climate negligence, climate denial,* and *climate lobbyism* presented in combination with non-verbal cues such as images and films of climatic phenomena, statistics presented in tables and graphs, eyewitness reports, and so on. The exact understanding of these names and other cues, on the other hand, is in itself highly dependent on the framings in which they occur and how communicators use them for framing each other.

Figure 4.1 shows a somewhat simplistic but hopefully illustrative visualization of the interplay between all four levels of naming & framing in relation to the topic (and name) *climate change*, expanding on the right-hand part of Figure 0.1.

In sum, the four levels of naming & framing suggested in this book are intimately connected and in constant interplay with each other, forming what might be called an ecosystem of naming & framing processes. Like any ecosystem, it remains in a state of permanent evolution which, to a wide extent, is driven by competition between its current elements.

The latter point connects further to Entman's considerations about target audiences. Depending on what "camp" one is in, using a particular name and/or displaying different understandings of the same name may influence the communicator's credibility with a given audience or even eliminate his or her chances of being understood at all. Apart from *climate change*, clear examples of this are *premenstrual syndrome, e-cigarettes,* and *information war*, which were all discussed earlier. The ultimate consequence is the formation of what some authors call information (or filter) bubbles as supported by such psychological mechanisms as avoidance of

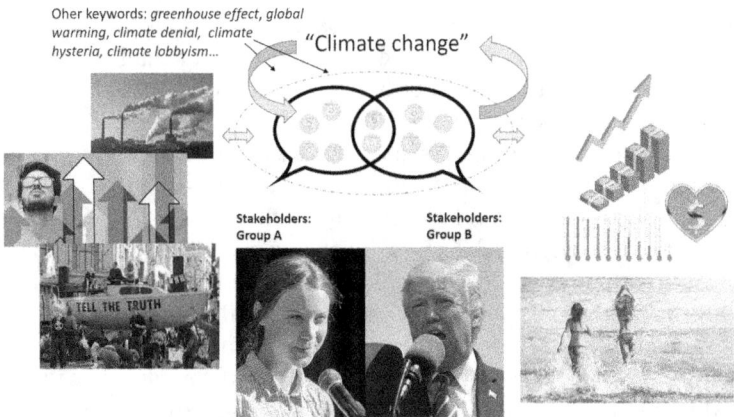

Figure 4.1 The full ecosystem of naming and faming processes illustrated by the current climate change debate.

cognitive dissonance; see Sections 2.2, 3.2.2, and 4.5. What the present analysis may add to these insights is that the struggle for definitional power in public space, even when it comes to single words, seems to continue within the mind of each single individual. This adds new relevance to what was predicted by Putnam's (1975a,b) hypothesis of division of linguistic labour and finds partial empirical support in experimental findings so far restricted to the sphere of food naming (Smith et al., 2013) but with potential implications also for other societal domains; see Section 3.3. For a related point formulated from a somewhat different philosophical standpoint, see Sommers-Flanagan & Sommers-Flanagan (2018: 283–310).

4.4 Implications for Communicative Ethics and Fairness

The above considerations lead us further to the issue of communicative ethics. Entman and many other authors with him take a critical stance on the competitive advantages that powerful communicators, whether political or commercial, tend to gain over less powerful ones in diffusing interest-driven framings, and the poor job that (some) news media and other expectable watchdogs of the general public allegedly do to ensure a better balance (Entman, 2007; 2004; 2003; 1993: 55–57; see also e.g. Kabel, 2017; Kellner, 2015; Reese, 2010; Miller & Dinan, 2008; Kumar, 2006; Druckman &

Parkin, 2005; Pollack, 2004; for a business perspective, see also e.g. Jones, 2014; Bone & France, 2001; Balasubramanian, 1994). Since the 1990s, the rise of the Internet and the social media has opened new opportunities for a better balanced and more critical interaction, but also new pitfalls, including a still more blurring borderline between paid, earned, shared, and owned media (Knüpfer & Entman, 2018; Macnamara, Lwin, Adi, & Zerfass, 2016) in a still more polyphonic media landscape (Castelló, Morsing, & Schultz, 2013); see also Section 3.2.2.

As a response to these developments, professional communicators and their organizations tend to put still more emphasis on responsible conduct and self-regulation adhering to criteria such as truthfulness, transparency, accountability, and compliance with legal regulations (PRSA, 2018; CIPR, 2018). Concordantly, the body of national and supranational legislation directly addressing the borderline between fair and potentially misleading communication is also growing, in particular with regard to commercial communicative practices such as advertising, product labelling, and e-commerce. However, legislators and courts have also repeatedly been criticized for prioritizing immediately measurable criteria such as documentation of factual correctness while neglecting the more subtle communicative pitfalls that emerge from the psychological specifics of human information processing and decision-making (Jones, 2014; Trzaskowski, 2011; Smith, Møgelvang-Hansen, & Hyldig, 2010; Incardona & Poncibò, 2007; Wansink & Shandon, 2006; Bone & France, 2001).

For example, in a critical analysis of the Unfair Commercial Practices Directive (UCPD, 2005/29/EC) which constitutes the regulatory foundation of consumer-oriented business communications and sales promotion in the European Union, Trzaskowski, (2011) substantiates at some length that the provisions of the UCPD and, even more so, the detailed legislation and court practices implementing them canonize an idealized understanding of the notorious benchmark character labelled "the average consumer." Disclosing a strong influence from economic theorizing, the result is a consistently rational Homo Economicus who is assumed to compare the value of all options faced in daily life and then follow the best possible path of action. Trzakowski argues that these expectations are directly contradicted by an extensive body of empirical research on consumer behaviour and human decision-making (to which we return shortly) which suggests that people routinely compromise on their rationality under influence of factors such as limitations in time and cognitive capacity, degree of perceived importance, reliance on repetitions, spontaneous emotional responses, and so on (see also Gidlöf, Wallin, Holmqvist, & Møgelvang-Hansen, 2013; Kahneman, 2011; Ariely, 2008; Incardona & Poncibò, 2007). Trzakowski argues that such insights can be and will eventually need to be better accommodated in running legislative and administrative practices. However, considering that the whole issue is only gradually beginning to emerge as a discussion topic in its own right in the mainstream legal literature, no quick fix seems to be in sight at present (cf. Conradie, 2016: 4).

What is perhaps more striking, and potentially a bit disturbing, is the fact that professional communicators' emphasis on criteria such as truthfulness, transparency, etc. (see above) is equally insufficient to cope with the challenge. Professional communicators should be the first to know that factually correct information can be presented (framed) in ways that support interest-driven interpretations at the expense of other, equally plausible ones, and that knowing and trusting a source do not guarantee that it will always tell you the only conceivable story or one that all interested parties would consider to be the most relevant one. Several examples discussed so far illustrate this (for further discussion, see also Dynel, 2016; Carson, 2016). What tends to get lost in the debate about law and ethics, then, is the existence of obvious psychological reasons why framing works, both with ordinary citizens and expectable watchdogs of the public, and that the very fact of being able to control these mechanisms is an integral part of the professional competence and job descriptions of strategic communicators at the operational level. Before taking these considerations further, let us therefore briefly sum up some of the most widely recognized mechanisms involved, and also consider how communicators' concrete choices of verbal and non-verbal communicative means are likely to interact with them.

4.5 Why Framing Works

At the risk of oversimplification, the psychological mechanisms of relevance can be subsumed under two main headings: reliance on stereotypes and a tendency towards mental shortcuts. Both have been approached from a variety of theoretical end empirical perspectives and with great variations in terminology. We will consider them, in turn, and, on that background, introduce the approach of relevance theory (RT) which connects the cognitive consequences of the mechanisms mentioned more directly to communicators' choice and combination of multimodal communicative resources.

4.5.1 Stereotype Thinking

It is well documented that the immense complexity of perceived reality leads people to resort to stereotypes[4] of various sorts, i.e. simplified mental "templates" which summarize past experiences for future use, be it when ordering food in a restaurant, discussing home duties with teenagers, or evaluating candidates for an election. Different manifestations of these mechanisms have been investigated in further depth under a variety of headings such as stereotypes (Fiske & Taylor, 2013; Hilton & von Hippel, 1996), mental models (Fairhurst, 2011; Johnson-Laird, 2006), scripts (Singh, Barry, & Liu, 2004; Schank, 1999), schemas (or schemata) (Hampe & Grady, 2005; Rumelhart, 1980), narratives (Rideout, 2008; Bruner, Hinchman, & Hinchman, 1997), and, indeed, frames (Cienki, 2007; Kittay & Lehrer, 1992). The latter use of the term *frame* thus adds yet another layer to its inherent ambiguity in that it both covers the communicative means used for activating a particular (stereotypical) understanding of a given situation and that understanding itself (for a clear separation of the two uses of the term, see Scheufele, 1999). Successful framing (in the sense of choice of communicative means) thus often relies on activating one set of stereotypical expectations at the expense of others, leaving the remaining gaps to be filled out by the recipients, thus unknowingly finishing the job of the communicator. To take an example of a less fortunate decision in that regard considered a couple of times earlier: The failure of the Danish political initiative termed *betalingsring* (lit. ≈ 'payment ring') can be explained as an unintentional activation of the stereotype 'politicians seeking new tax revenues' instead of the intended

---

4 In the frameworks considered in this section, the term *stereotype* and the partially overlapping term *prototype* are often understood in a more inclusive sense than the ones adopted, for instance, by Putnam (see Section 3.3) and Rosch (see Section 1.3) who specifically refer to the conceptual structures conveyed by single words. Thus, apart from its pivotal role in lexical semantics, thinking in stereotypes also appears to be a major factor in our mental handling of more complex real-life scenarios (e.g. dining at restaurants) that are thematically related to the meaning of a variety of words (e.g. *waiter, table, menu, course, drink, bill, tips*, and (potentially) *romance* or *overeating*). For further discussion on the different levels of stereotype thinking and their treatment in different traditions of research, see Cienki (2007).

'politicians responding to environmental challenges,' as triggered, in this case, by the morphological motivation of the name itself (i.e. by naming & framing at Level 2, but with consequences also for Levels 3 and 4).

4.5.2 Mental Shortcuts

The effect can be further enhanced by mental shortcuts. In our daily lives, we are confronted with an abundance of choices, and dealing exhaustingly with each of them far exceeds our mental capacity (Kahneman, 2011; Schwartz, 2004; Petty & Cacioppo, 1986). We are therefore predisposed to elaborate more on some decisions than on others depending on their perceived importance.

One much quoted theoretical framework that addresses this phenomenon in operational terms is the elaboration likelihood model first proposed by Petty & Cacioppo (1986; see O'Keefe, 2016: 148–175 for further developments). The model distinguishes between a central processing route for high-involvement decision-making (say, buying a house or undergoing risky surgery) where complex information is actively sought and compared, and a peripheral route for low-involvement decision-making (say, buying a frozen dinner or deciding whether to believe in tabloid media's accusations of sexual harassment against some less known politician) where the decision-making is based on a smaller number of random cues such as attractive packaging design, a single convincing argument, or plain trust in the communicator. In turn, this paves the ground for so-called halo effects (Forgas, & Laham, 2016; Chandon & Wansink, 2007; Nisbett & Wilson, 1977), i.e. unwarranted additional inferences consistent with the positive or negative judgement initially derived from the cues actually considered (say, expecting that a product which carries an organic-farming label is also low on fat or that a politician accused of sexual harassment must be an anti-feminist).

4.5.3 A Quest for Situational Relevance

While the generation of such potentially misguided inferences on the background of factually not incorrect (but often scarce) information has been extensively observed and described (see also e.g. Peterson & Palmer, 2017; Lähteenmäki et al., 2010; Roe, Levy, & Derby, 1999), fewer frameworks take the analysis beyond acknowledging, on a generic level, the important role played by psychological mechanisms such as those mentioned in determining the final outcome. That is, the observations are not always followed up by more detailed hypothesizing about exactly which justified or misguided (including deliberately misleading) inferences a communicator may induce in the recipient by choosing particular constellations of verbal and non-verbal communicative means in preference to others for conveying the intended message.

A possible scheme for such an operational analysis is offered by RT which was originally proposed by Sperber & Wilson (1995; see also Wilson & Sperber, 2012) with a primary focus on the implicit dimension of sense-making during interpersonal language-based communication, but later transposed also to the analysis of mass communication and the interplay between visual and verbal communicative resources (Forceville, 2014, 2008; Cummings, 2013; Taillard, 2000).

The gist of the theory is that any information that a communicator brings to the communicative scene will be expected by the recipient[5] to be relevant to the situation in which it is uttered in one way or another. If the relevance is not clear to the recipient from what is said explicitly (called explicatures in RT terminology), (s)he will initiate a subconscious process of step-by-step relevance processing by matching the explicit information with information already accessible to him or her while tentatively adding (inferring) pieces of new information at his/her own risk that might establish a sensible connection between the two (called implicatures in RT terminology, i.e. presumed messages not explicitly articulated by the communicator). Stated more plainly, the recipient will try to answer the question "why are you telling me this?" until some plausible explanation comes to mind. The process stops when the cost of additional relevance processing exceeds the expected cognitive benefit in terms of new knowledge that can be used efficiently in the situation. In low-involvement settings such as everyday shopping or reading gossip pages, that point can be expected to be reached relatively fast (see Section 4.5.2). Moreover, different recipients may have access to different types and levels of knowledge, yielding equally different results (see Figure 4.2a and b).

---

5 If we take the multimodal perspective into account, it might be added that such expectations are likely to be further enhanced if the corresponding expression-units are visually highlighted, suggesting to the recipient that this is something that the sender finds it particularly important to communicate. One example would be a "splash" containing a low-fat claim on the front of a product package as shown in Figure 4.2a/b. For further discussion on the interplay between bottom-up (stimulus-driven) and top-down (goal-driven) attention during the decoding of multimodal communicative products, see Section 3.2.1.

Naming & Framing at Level 4 71

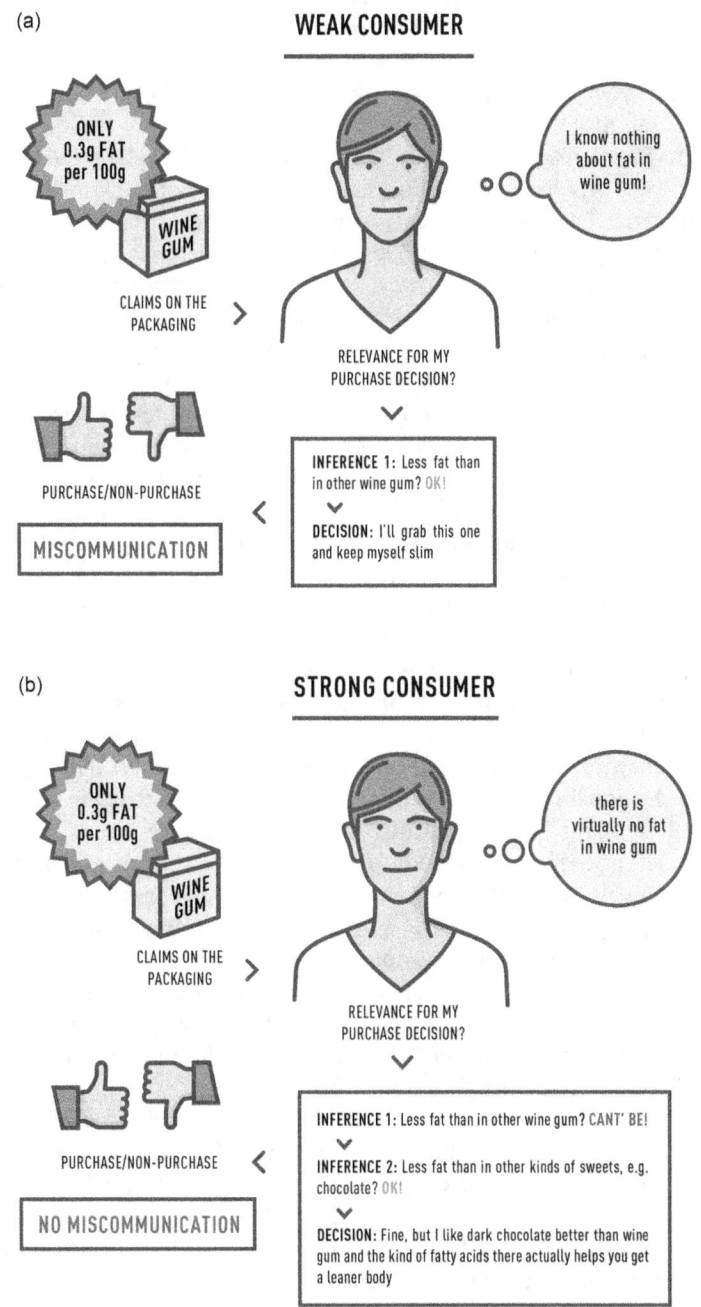

Figure 4.2 Relevance processing: the case of wine gum.

To illustrate, let us once again consider the condensed "cocktails" of semiotic resources found on product packages. In an authentic legal dispute (among the 821 cases covered by the case review presented in Smith, Clement, Møgelvang-Hansen, & Selsøe Sørensen, 2011; see also Møgelvang-Hansen, 2010), the visually highlighted claim *Kun 0,3% fedt pr. 100 g* ('Only 0.3% fat per 100 g') on the front of a pack of wine gum was ultimately banned by the Danish food authorities because it was considered likely that consumers would expect the product to contain less fat than other types of wine gum which was not the case. However, throughout the proceedings, the manufacturer insisted that the relevant comparison (if any) was not with wine gum at all, but with other types of sweets among which, say, chocolate or marzipan contain much more fat. Characteristically, the case was never subject to any empirical testing (see also Section 4.4), but the relevance-theoretical approach allows us to hypothesize a bit further on the validity of the respective arguments.

Thus, a consumer with minimal knowledge of health and nutrition issues (classified as a weak consumer in some contexts) may well stop the relevance processing at the point suggested in Figure 4.2a and be utterly misled. By contrast, a consumer with more extensive knowledge of health and nutrition issues (classified as a strong consumer in the same contexts) is likely to continue the relevance processing beyond that point. Indeed, (s)he is likely to reach a conclusion similar to the one allegedly intended by the manufacturer all along. However, this does not necessarily mean that the consumer will also take the line of action that the manufacturer might have hoped for. In having access to extensive and diverse knowledge of food and nutrition issues, the consumer may continue his or her decision-making in several directions, including the one suggested in Figure 4.2b. None of this alters the circumstance that a less knowledgeable, or simply less involved, recipient will be at a substantial risk of being misled. Provision of harder empirical evidence to underpin legal decisions in such grey-zone cases is thus an obvious subject for further research, and experimental work along these lines is presently in progress.

Another issue relative to which RT would seem to have a not yet fully fulfilled explanatory potential is the question of how situational inference-making triggered by images differs from that triggered by words (cf. Forceville, 2014, 2008). As earlier observed by Messaris (1997), a key difference between picture-based and language-based communication is that pictures are propositionally (syntactically) indeterminate, that is, they may well refer to something beyond themselves (by resembling it, i.e. as an instance of iconicity), but lack the formal means to make explicit propositional statements about that something that could be assessed in terms of true or false. Take a photo of a pile of fresh raspberries as compared to the verbal statement "contains 0,2% raspberry concentrate" on a tub of yoghurt.

As a consequence, *any* situational decoding of pictures must ultimately rely on ad-hoc inference-making (i.e. a search for implicatures to state it in the RT terms mentioned earlier) since no explicit statements (explicatures) can be conveyed by a picture in the first place. However, Forceville (2014) argues that a two-layered analysis is nevertheless both possible and required, illustrating his point by a cartoon panel (containing no words) from a Tintin story by Hergé. What one sees immediately can thus still be transposed into an explicit propositional statement such as "Tintin and Snowy walk toward a hut in a forest" (corresponding to the level of explicatures in language-based communication). However, to grasp what exactly that information contributes to the overall story, additional inferences are needed (corresponding to the level of implicatures in language-based communication).

To return once again to the communicative impact of product packaging design: It is widely assumed by the authorities and courts of many countries that a photo of a potentially taste-giving ingredient shown on the packaging of a food product will lead consumers to expect that the taste in question stems (primarily) from that ingredient and not from artificial flavouring, rendering the opposite case one of potentially misleading food labelling. By contrast, judgements tend to be more liberal if the corresponding taste is "only" suggested by isolated words such as *raspberry* or *sour cream & onion* or by a stylized drawing.[6] An experimental study

---

6 An essential circumstance not covered by Messaris' (1997) considerations about the differences between language-based and picture-based communication mentioned earlier is that isolated words are just as propositionally indetermined as pictures. Thus, the word *raspberry* could be taken to mean 'contains raspberries,' 'tastes of raspberries,' 'shaped like a raspberry' (in the case of a toy), 'has a raspberry fragrance' (in the case of a shampoo), 'produces raspberries' (in the case of seeds), and so on. Indeed, in the regulatory contexts just mentioned, photos seem to be understood as *less* propositionally indeterminate than words, i.e. as favouring a straightforward reading in terms of actual content. The circumstance that this reasoning is not automatically extended to

designed to shed empirical light on these pre-theoretical assumptions (Smith, Barratt, & Sørensen, 2015) demonstrated that the presence of a photo did indeed enhance consumers' expectations about the natural origin of the taste in question to a small, but statistically significant, degree. However, the effect of product type was far more prominent. The participants were more optimistic about finding real beef in beef bouillon than about finding real fruit in fruit candy, photo or not. Furthermore, participants with a relatively low level of knowledge on food and nutrition issues (assessed in a separate questionnaire) tended to be more optimistic about naturalness in general than those with a higher knowledge level.

Forceville's (2014) approach offers some additional leads to explaining such findings. To start with the level of close-to-propositional "literal" readings (corresponding to explicatures in language-based communication), the circumstance that the pictures in fact did have an effect on some participants even for expectedly less-natural products may come down to the fact that a reading in terms of 'contains X' is cognitively less demanding than a reading in terms of 'contains artificial flavouring reproducing the flavour of X.' Thus, some less knowledgeable and/or involved participants may simply have settled for the easiest possible solution and not taken their relevance processing further than that. A potentially contributing factor (which leads the analysis on to what corresponds to implicatures in language-based communication) is that showing a photo instead of merely using the corresponding word could be taken, relevance-wise, as an indication of "the real thing" actually being present in the product (see also Messaris, 1997, notion of photographic indexicality which he describes as a major tool for suggesting real-world existence commonly used in advertising and news media, even if increasingly compromised by easy access to still more convincing image manipulation tools in present-day digital media; for further discussion on the latter point, see Messaris, 2012).

---

drawings might, in turn, come down to their more conventionalized character which allows more generalized and abstract readings as may also be argued for words. The real-life communicative domain addressed in the experimental study to be summarized here offers a suitable context for testing such assumptions against empirical observations, even if some variables of interest, including the photo-drawing opposition, remain to be additionally scrutinized in future work.

Be that as it may, the majority of participants appear to have been sufficiently knowledgeable and/or involved to reject the simplest accessible proposition-like reading and consider other alternatives. Moreover, the presence of a photo in itself may also have been interpreted differently, say, as an indication that the manufacturer wants the consumer to *believe* that the product contains that ingredient, which is not tantamount to believing it oneself. While hypothetical at this stage, such considerations might well be put to further empirical test in the future. Furthermore, on top of possible propositional interpretations comes the well-documented circumstance that the decoding of pictures involves the same neural systems that we use to detect actual objects and events which, in turn, are closely connected to other systems via associative connections (Vermeulen, Corneille, & Niedenthal, 2008; Beauchamp, Lee, Haxby, & Martin, 2002; Damasio & Damasio, 1994), including those underlying taste and reward (Simmons, Martin, & Barsalou, 2005). This means that seeing a picture of what one knows to be a tasty ingredient may elicit a spontaneous emotional desire for the corresponding sensory experience, bypassing any more elaborate information processing that might otherwise have preceded the purchase decision. In sum, placing pictures of natural ingredients on products not containing them has a versatile potential for compromising communicative fairness even if it is hard to accuse anyone of "lying" about anything.

4.6 Is Fair (Strategic) Communication Possible?

Returning to persuasive communication in general and the ample possibilities offered by a number of psychological mechanisms to support it (some of which were just considered in further detail), one question remains: Where does all this leave communicative fairness – and is such an ideal feasible at all? Some authors argue to the contrary (Gidlöf et al., 2013), while others opt for a more balanced approach (Smith et al., 2011). Thus, none of what has been said so far alters the fact that *some* individuals will on *some* occasions demonstrably try to dig deeper into whatever subject has caught their particular interest, given realistic time constraints and the prior knowledge available to them. What can reasonably be expected of fairness-minded communicators, then, would be to keep all doors open to such an honest attempt rather than systematically obscuring it, which is by no means tantamount to abstaining from promoting whatever good cause one might have.

Addressing the still more heated debates on whether cyberspace promotes democracy and human rights or leaves such institutions open to attack from less democratically minded actors, Tabansky (2017, 2013) suggests applying Karl Popper's falsifiability principle to evaluating research results of potential relevance. The principle says, in short, that any hypothesis should be formulated in a way so that it can be tested against alternative hypotheses and declared false if not consistent with the evidence gained. Tabansky's primary concern is thus with defining the scientific "rules of the game" for feeding into political debates which, arguably, entails a certain risk of politicalizing the scientific debate itself. At least, a complementary perspective would be to see citizens' awareness of and uncompromised access to examining and critically comparing alternative framings of any issue of their potential interest as a fundamental precondition of any informed opinion-building, perhaps for the exception of messages that violate fundamental democratic principles such as promotion of racism or child abuse. In developed democracies, this ideal is no longer threatened by overt censorship (for political messages) or lack of efficient legal regulation of evidently dishonest conducts such as lying and cheating (for commercial messages), but by the obvious potential of powerful communicators to promote some interest-driven framings at the direct expense of others, as backed up by humans' deep-rooted tendency to rely on stereotype thinking, low-involvement decision-making, unsubstantiated inferences, and avoidance of cognitive dissonance (see Entman, 1993: 56–58 for closely related concerns not yet envisaging the rise of cyberspace).

What could be done to remedy this situation is far beyond the scope of this book. However, recognizing and understanding the totality of mechanisms involved would appear to be a good start.

5 Concluding Remarks

Most of the theoretical frameworks addressed in this book are not new in themselves. However, many of them have not previously been combined or applied to the elaborate patchwork of issues that we have here subsumed under the heading of naming & framing. Likewise, many of the practical areas of human activity where the power of words is recognized as a decisive factor (marketing, politics, journalism, health care, terminology management, and so on) are highly selective about which analytical and operational tools they allow into their own remit, leaving potentially fruitful cross-disciplinary synergies unattended.

So far, the most prominent focus in research published under the present heading is naming & framing in the inclusive sense here referred to as Level 4. However, the operationalization of this level goes through what we have called Levels 1–3, that is, selecting and/or creating and contextually framing particular names in a way that underpins particular strategic or intuitive agendas. This includes operating on the mechanisms through which a particular understanding of a given wider subject becomes encapsulated (also) in individual names and enrolled in something as seemingly objective and monolithic as human language(s). In other words, we are dealing with an ecosystem where all four levels feed into each other, and although the interest in the mainstream framing literature presently tends to "get stuck" at Level 4, the lasting effect will usually be fixed at Level 1 (via 2 and 3), which is how we can explain why many people support *ecotaxes*, recent *propaganda*, and like *Apple* computers.

Manoeuvring across this whole ecosystem is nowadays mostly left to communicative practitioners who rely primarily on their accumulated hands-on experience, talent, and intuition. However, the present account shows that several fields of research so far unattended in a declared naming & framing context have essential insights and tools to contribute to this work.

That includes theorizing and empirical evidence on:

- the degree to which the structural and typological features of individual languages may constrain or support particular naming & framing decisions and strategies;
- the dynamic nature of human categorization, including the role of situational, social, and cultural factors in determining whether or not a given category is likely to become canonized and "frozen" by language;
- people's real-time decoding of familiar names and spontaneous interpretation of unfamiliar (novel) names in running communication, including the specifics of non-arbitrary (motivated) names in this respect;
- the interplay between the built-in semantic potential of a name (viz. the Joyce principle) and the influence of surrounding verbal and nonverbal contextual cues (viz. the Juliet principle) that ultimately determines the name's full communicative potential;
- competing framings of the same name in running communication and how they influence individual language users' personal understanding and use of that name in different situations, as captured by the hypothesis of division of linguistic labour;
- people's real-time decoding of multimodal communicative products encountered in still more complex transmedial environments, including the dynamics between visual attention and semantic disambiguation and the influence of different processing patterns in that regard on people's comprehension of individual names and of more complex subject matters;
- the impact of different constellations of verbal and nonverbal communicative resources on people's inference-making during situational relevance processing and how different outcomes of these processes may affect emotions, beliefs, and subsequent decision-making.

It is hard to see how a comprehensive understanding of our present topic could be reached without including (at least) the perspectives just mentioned. And yet, they tend to live their separate lives in different disciplines, research communities, journals, collaborative projects, organizations, and so on. Attempts to bridge between (some of) them have nevertheless repeatedly been made and some are taken a step further in this book in pursuing the overall agenda set up in Section 0.3. The circumstance that this does not appear to be entirely infeasible, if one decides to try, suggests that the perspectives are complementary rather than inherently alien.

What is needed most of all is a good cause, and in that respect taking a genuine interest in real-life communicative domains and resultant communicative products viewed (also) in their entirety rather than breaking them down into smaller parts and sub-issues from the outset appears to be an effective catalyst. The overarching agenda of multimodal communication research is probably the most clear example of the potential of such a more holistic approach to enhance our understanding also of specific sub-issues such as (in casu) naming & framing operations. The same is, of course, true of the domains of human activity in which they occur. Real-life naming & framing decisions made in the course of promoting new products, setting political agendas, or fighting gender inequality at ones workplaces are bound to involve some – even if often intuitive – consideration about which words will do the job best, how the verbal and visual surroundings in which they are used will affect people's comprehension of them, and to what degree the intended message is consistent with the current conceptual landscape of the intended audience.

The modest ambition of this book is to bring a broader selection of theoretical insights and analytical tools into "active duty" in such domains where naming and framing decisions are in fact being made and/or evaluated on a daily basis. In turn, the establishment of such new links would seem to have a potential for feeding new impulses back into the contributing disciplines themselves and diversifying the cross-disciplinary dialogue between them. Furthermore, some of the points and observations made might also be brought to bear in current debates on communicative ethics and fairness, qualifying miscommunication as much more than a matter of factual (in)correctness.

References

Aaker, D. (1991). *Managing brand equity: Capitalizing on the value of a brand name.* The Free Press.

Agyemang, C., Bhopal, R., & Bruijnzeels, M. (2005). Negro, Black, Black African, African Caribbean, African American or what? Labelling African origin populations in the health arena in the 21st century. *Journal of Epidemiology & Community Health*, 59(12), 1014–1018.

Aitchison, J. (2012). *Words in the mind: An introduction to the mental lexicon.* Fourth edition. John Wiley & Sons.

Alexander, C. (2017). New study comes the closest yet to proving that e-cigarettes aren't as dangerous as smoking. *Cancer Research UK.* URL: https://scienceblog.cancerresearchuk.org/2017/02/06/new-study-comes-the-closest-yet-to-proving-that-e-cigarettes-arent-as-dangerous-as-smoking/ (accessed June 2020).

Alexander, D., Lynch, J., & Wang, Q. (2008). As time goes by: Warm intentions and cold feet for really new versus incrementally new products. *Journal of Marketing Research*, 45(3), 307–319.

Anderson, W. B. (2018). Counter-framing: Implications for public relations. *Public Relations Inquiry*, 7(2), 111–126.

Andrews, S., & Davis, C. (1999). Interactive activation accounts of morphological decomposition: Finding the trap in mousetrap? *Brain and Language*, 68(1–2), 355–361.

Ang, S. H. (1997). Chinese consumers' perception of alpha-numeric brand names. *Journal of Consumer Marketing*, 14(3), 220–233.

Apthorpe, R., & Gasper, D. (Eds.). (1996). *Arguing development policy: Frames and discourses.* Routledge.

Ares, G., Giménez, A., Bruzzone, F., Vidal, L., Antúnez, L., & Maiche, A. (2013). Consumer visual processing of food labels: Results from an eye-tracking study. *Journal of Sensory Studies*, 28(2), 38–153.

Ariel, M. (2010). *Defining pragmatics.* Cambridge University Press.

Ariely, D. (2008). *Predictably irrational.* Harper Collins.

Armstrong, J. (2016). The problem of lexical innovation. *Linguistics and Philosophy*, 39(2), 87–118.

Arora, S., Kalro, A. D., & Sharma, D. (2015). A comprehensive framework of brand name classification. *Journal of Brand Management*, 22(2), 79–116.

References

Avineri, E., & Waygood, E. O. D. (2013). Applying valence framing to enhance the effect of information on transport-related carbon dioxide emissions. *Transportation Research Part A: Policy and Practice*, 48, 31–38.

Backhaus, J. G. (1999). The law and economics of environmental taxation: When should the ecotax kick in? *International Review of Law and Economics*, 19(1), 117–134.

Bail, C. A. (2014). The cultural environment: Measuring culture with big data. *Theory and Society*, 43(3–4), 465–482.

Balasubramanian, S. K. (1994). Beyond advertising and publicity: Hybrid messages and public policy issues. *Journal of Advertising*, 23(4), 29–46.

Baldinger, K. (1980). *Semantic theory: Towards a modern semantics*. Blackwell.

Banyard, K. (2016). The dangers of rebranding prostitution as 'sex work.' *The Guardian*. June 7, 2016. URL: https://www.theguardian.com/lifeandstyle/2016/jun/06/prostitution-sex-work-pimp-state-kat-banyard-decriminalisation (accessed June 2020).

Barsalou, L. W. (2016). Situated conceptualization: Theory and applications. In Y. Coello & M. H. Fischer (Eds.), *Foundations of embodied cognition, Volume 1: Perceptual and emotional embodiment* (pp. 11–37). Psychology Press.

Barsalou, L. W. (2010). Grounded cognition: Past, present, and future. *Topics in Cognitive Science*, 2(4), 716–724.

Barsalou, L. W. (2003). Situated simulation in the human conceptual system. *Language and Cognitive Processes*, 18(5–6), 513–562.

Barsalou, L. W. (1995). Deriving categories to achieve goals. In A. Ram & D. B. Leake (Eds.), *Goal Directed Learning* (pp. 121–176). MIT Press.

Barsalou, L. W. (1987). The instability of graded structure: Implications for the nature of concepts. In U. Neisser (Ed.), *Concepts and conceptual development: Ecological and intellectual factors in categorization* (pp. 101–140). Cambridge University Press.

Barsalou, L. W. (1983). Ad hoc categories. *Memory & Cognition*, 11(3), 211–227.

Barton, H. (2016). Persuasion and compliance in cyberspace In I. Connolly, M. Palmer, H. Barton, & G. Kirwan (Eds.), *An introduction to cyberpsychology* (pp. 111–123). Routledge.

BBC News. (2018). Syria war: What we know about Douma 'chemical attack'. *BBC News*. July 10, 2018. URL: https://www.bbc.com/news/world-middle-east-43697084 (accessed June 2020).

Beauchamp, M. S., Lee, K. E., Haxby, J. V., & Martin, A. (2002). Parallel visual motion processing streams for manipulable objects and human movements. *Neuron*, 34(1), 149–159.

Benczes, R. (2006a). Analysing metonymical noun-noun compounds: The case of freedom fries. *The metaphors of sixty: Papers presented on the occasion of the 60th birthday of Zoltán Kövecses*, 46–54.

Benczes, R. (2006b). *Creative compounding in English. The semantics of metaphorical and metonymical noun-noun combinations.* John Benjamins.
Bentsen, S. E. (2018). *The comprehension of English texts by native speakers of English, and Japanese, Chinese and Russian speakers of English as a Lingua Franca: An empirical study.* PhD Thesis. Copenhagen Business School.
Berger, J. (2014). Word of mouth and interpersonal communication: A review and directions for future research. *Journal of Consumer Psychology*, 24(4), 586–607.
Berlin, B., & Kay, P. (1969). *Basic color terms: Their universality and evolution.* University of California Press.
Berridge, V. (1996). *AIDS in the UK: The making of policy, 1981–1994.* Oxford University Press.
Berthele, R., & Stocker, L. (2016). The effect of language mode on motion event descriptions in German–French bilinguals. *Language and Cognition*, 9(4), 648–676.
BibleGateway. (2011). The tower of Babel. Genesis 11: 1–9. New International Version (NIV). *BibleGateway.* URL: https://www.biblegateway.com/passage/?search=Genesis+11%3A1-9&version=NIV (accessed June 2020).
Birkbak, A. (2017). When financial concerns shape traffic policy: How economic assumptions muted the Copenhagen payment zone issue. *Science as Culture*, 26(4), 491–504.
Bizer, G. Y., & Petty, R. E. (2005). How we conceptualize our attitudes matters: The effects of valence framing on the resistance of political attitudes. *Political Psychology*, 26(4), 553–568.
Blank, S., & Dorf, B. (2012). *The startup owner's manual: The step-by-step guide for building a great company.* K & S Ranch.
Boas, F. (1911). *Handbook of American Indian languages.* Nabu Press.
Böck, M., & Pachler, N. (Eds.). (2013). *Multimodality and social semiosis: Communication, meaning-making, and learning in the work of Gunther Kress.* Routledge.
Bone, P. F., & France, K. R. (2001). Package graphics and consumer product beliefs. *Journal of Business and Psychology*, 15(3), 467–489.
Bovaird, T. (2004). Public–private partnerships: From contested concepts to prevalent practice. *International Review of Administrative Sciences*, 70(2), 199–215.
Brown, F. C., Buboltz, Jr, W. C., & Soper, B. (2002). Relationship of sleep hygiene awareness, sleep hygiene practices, and sleep quality in university students. *Behavioral Medicine*, 28(1), 33–38.
Brown, P. (1995). Naming and framing: The social construction of diagnosis and illness. *Journal of Health and Social Behavior*, 35(Extra Issue), 34–52.
Bruner, E. M., Hinchman, L. P., & Hinchman, S. K. (1997). *Memory, identity, community: The Idea of narrative in the human sciences.* State University of New York Press.

Bruni, E., Tran, N. K., & Baroni, M. (2014). Multimodal distributional semantics. *Journal of Artificial Intelligence Research*, 49, 1–47.

Bulling, A. (2016). Pervasive attentive user interfaces. *IEEE Computer*, 49(1), 94–98.

Busse, D. (2017). Frames as a model for the analysis and description of concepts, conceptual structures, conceptual change, and concept hierarchies. In T. Pommerening & W. Bisang (Eds.), *Classification from antiquity to modern times* (pp. 281–309). De Gruyter Mouton.

Bybee, J. (2007). *Frequency of use and the organization of language.* Oxford University Press.

Bybee, J. (1995). Regular morphology and the lexicon. *Language and Cognitive Processes*, 10(5), 425–455.

Carey, C. (1994). Rhetorical means of persuasion. In I. Worthington (Ed.), *Persuasion: Greek rhetoric in action* (pp. 26–45). Routledge.

Carson, T. L. (2016). Frankfurt and Cohen on bullshit, bullshiting, deception, lying, and concern with the truth of what one says. *Pragmatics & Cognition*, 23(1), 53–67.

Castelló, I., Morsing, M., & Schultz, F. (2013). Communicative dynamics and the polyphony of corporate social responsibility in the network society. *Journal of Business Ethics*, 118(4), 683–694.

Chan, A. K. K., & Huang, Y. Y. (2001). Chinese brand naming: A linguistic analysis of the brands of ten product categories. *Journal of Product & Brand Management*, 10(2), 103–119.

Chandon, P., & Wansink, B. (2007). The biasing health halos of fast-food restaurant health claims: Lower calorie estimates and higher side-dish consumption intentions. *Journal of Consumer Research*, 34(3), 301–314.

Chang, W. L., & Lii, P. (2008). Luck of the draw: Creating Chinese brand names. *Journal of Advertising Research*, 48(4), 523–530.

Charette, P., Hooker, N. H., & Stanton, J. L. (2015). Framing and naming: A process to define a novel food category. *Food Quality and Preference*, 40, 147–151.

Charteris-Black, J. (2011). *Politicians and rhetoric: The persuasive power of metaphor.* Palgrave Macmillan.

Chong, D., & Druckman, J. N. (2007). Framing theory. *Annual Review of Political Science*, 10, 103–126.

Chun, M. M., & Wolfe, J. M. (2008). Visual attention. In E. B. Goldstein (Ed.), *Blackwell handbook of sensation and perception* (pp. 272–310). Blackwell.

Cienki, A. (2007). Frames, idealized cognitive models, and domains. In D. Geeraerts & H. Cuyckens (Eds.), *The Oxford handbook of cognitive linguistics* (pp. 170–187). Oxford University Press.

CIPR. (2018). CIPR Code of Conduct. *Chartered Institute of Public Relations* (UK). URL: https://www.cipr.co.uk/ethics (accessed June 2020).

Clark, E. V. (2018). Word meanings and semantic domains in acquisition. *Semantics in Language Acquisition*, 24, 21–43.

References

Clement, J. (2007). Visual influence on in-store buying decisions: An eye-track experiment on the visual influence of packaging design. *Journal of Marketing Management*, 23(9–10), 917–928.

Cohen, L. J. (1986). How is conceptual innovation possible? *Erkenntnis*, 25(2), 221–238.

Colby, D. C., & Cook, T. E. (1991). Epidemics and agendas: The politics of nightly news coverage of AIDS. *Journal of Health Politics, Policy and Law*, 16(2), 215–249.

Collins, L. (1977). A name to conjure with: A discussion of the naming of new brands. *European Journal of Marketing*, 11(5), 337–363.

Conradie, E. (2016). *The implications for consumer protection law in the European Union of behaviourally informed commercial practices*. Master Thesis. Lund University. URL: https://lup.lub.lu.se/student-papers/search/publication/8884364 (accessed June 2020).

Corcoran, N. (Ed.). (2013). *Communicating health: Strategies for health promotion*. Second Edition. Sage.

Crable, R. E., & Vibbert, S. L. (1985). Managing issues and influencing public policy. *Public Relations Review*, 11(2), 3–16.

Cui, G., Lui, H. K., & Guo, X. (2012). The effect of online consumer reviews on new product sales. *International Journal of Electronic Commerce*, 17(1), 39–58.

Cummings, L. (2013). *Pragmatics: A multidisciplinary perspective*. Routledge.

Damasio, A. R., & Damasio, H. (1994). Cortical systems for retrieval of concrete knowledge: The convergence zone framework. In C. Koch & J. L. Davis, (Eds.), *Large-scale neuronal theories of the brain* (pp. 61–74). MIT Press.

D'Angelo, P., & Kuypers, J. A. (Eds.). (2010). *Doing news framing analysis. Empirical and theoretical perspectives*. Routledge.

Darics, E., & Koller, V. (2017). *Language in business, language at work*. Palgrave.

Darley, W. K., Blankson, C., & Luethge, D. J. (2010). Toward an integrated framework for online consumer behavior and decision making process: A review. *Psychology & marketing*, 27(2), 94–116.

de Bessé, B. (1997). Terminological definitions. In S. E. Wright & G. Budin (Eds.), *Handbook of terminology management. Volume 1: Basic aspects of terminology management* (pp. 63–74). John Benjamins.

de Saussure, F. (2011 [1916]). *Course in general linguistics*. Columbia University Press.

Deutscher, G. (2010). *Through the language glass: Why the world looks different in other languages*. Metropolitan Books.

Devitt, M., & Sterelny, K. (1999). *Language and realty: An introduction to the philosophy of language*. MIT Press.

Di Francesco, L. (2013). 7 criteria for a great brand name. *Business 2 Community*. URL: https://www.business2community.com/branding/7-criteria-for-a-great-brand-name-0375307 (accessed June 2020).

Drews, S., & van den Bergh, J. C. (2016). What explains public support for climate policies? A review of empirical and experimental studies. *Climate Policy*, 16(7), 855–876.

Druckman, J. N., & Parkin, M. (2005). The impact of media bias: How editorial slant affects voters. *The Journal of Politics*, 67(4), 1030–1049.

Durst-Andersen, P. (2011). *Linguistic supertypes. A cognitive-semiotic theory of human communication*. De Gruyter Mouton.

Durst-Andersen, P. (1992). *Mental grammar: Russian aspect and related issues*. Slavica Publishers.

Durst-Andersen, P., Smith, V., & Nedergaard Thomsen, O. (2013). Towards a cognitive-semiotic typology of motion verbs. In C. Paradis J. Hudson, & U. Magnusson (Eds.), *The construal of spatial meaning: Windows into conceptual space* (pp. 190–222). Oxford University Press.

Dynel, M. (2016). On untruthfulness, its adversaries and strange bedfellows. *Pragmatics & Cognition*, 23(1), 1–15.

Elish, M. C., & Boyd, D. (2018). Situating methods in the magic of Big Data and AI. *Communication Monographs*, 85(1), 57–80.

Emke, I. (2000). Agents and structures: Journalists and the constraints on AIDS coverage, *Canadian Journal of Communication*, 25(3), 325–345.

Entman, R. M. (2007). Framing bias: Media in the distribution of power. *Journal of Communication*, 57(1), 163–173.

Entman, R. M. (2004). *Projections of power: Framing news, public opinion, and US foreign policy*. University of Chicago Press.

Entman, R. M. (2003). Cascading activation: Contesting the White House's frame after 9/11, *Political Communication*, 20(4), 415–432.

Entman, R. M. (1993). Framing: Toward clarification of a fractured paradigm. *Journal of Communication*, 43(4), 51–58.

Esser, F., Reinemann, C., & Fan, D. (2000). Spin doctoring in British and German election campaigns: How the press is being confronted with a new quality of political PR. *European Journal of Communication*, 15(2), 209–239.

Evans, V., & Green, M. (2006). *Cognitive linguistics: An introduction*. Edinburgh University Press.

Fairclough, N. (2013). *Critical discourse analysis: The critical study of language*. Second edition. Routledge.

Fairhurst, G. (2011). *The power of framing: Creating the language of leadership*. John Wiley & Sons.

Fairhurst, G., & Sarr, R. (1996). *The art of framing*. Jossey-Bass.

Fauconnier, G., & Lakoff, G. (2009). On metaphor and blending. *Cognitive Semiotics*, 5(1–2), 393–399.

Fauconnier, G., & Turner, M. (2003). *The way we think: Conceptual blending and the mind's hidden complexities*. Basic Books.

Fenko, A., Nicolaas, I., & Galetzka, M. (2018). Does attention to health labels predict a healthy food choice? An eye-tracking study. *Food Quality and Preference*, 69, 57–65.

Festinger, L. (1957). *A theory of cognitive dissonance*. Stanford University Press.

Figert, A. E. (2017). *Women and the ownership of PMS*. Routledge.
Fillmore, C. J., Kay, P., & O'Connor, M. C. (1988). Regularity and idiomaticity in grammatical constructions: The case of let alone. *Language*, 64(3), 501–538.
Fiske, S. T., & Taylor, S. E. (2013). *Social cognition: From brains to culture*. Second edition. Sage.
Fodor, J. A. (1975) *The language of thought*. Harvard University Press.
Fog, K., Budtz, C., & Yakaboylu, B. (2005). *Storytelling: Branding in practice*. Springer.
Forceville, C. (2014). Relevance Theory as model for analysing visual and multimodal communication. In D. Machin (Ed.), *Visual Communication* (pp. 51–70). Walter de Gruyter.
Forceville, C. (2008). Metaphor in pictures and multimodal representations. In R. W. Gibbs, Jr. (Ed.), *The Cambridge handbook of metaphor and thought* (462–482). Cambridge University Press.
Forgas, J. P., & Laham, S. M. (2016). Halo effects. In R. F. Pohl (Ed.), *Cognitive illusions: Intriguing phenomena in judgement, thinking and memory* (276–290). Psychology Press.
Gagné, C. L., & Spalding, T. L. (2006). Conceptual combination: Implications for the mental lexicon. In G. Libben & G. Jarema (Eds.), *The representation and processing of compound words* (pp. 145–168). Oxford University Press.
Gagné, C. L., Spalding, T. L., & Gorrie, M. C. (2005). Sentential context and the interpretation of familiar open-compounds and novel modifier-noun phrases. *Language and Speech*, 48(2), 203–219.
Gallie, W. B. (1955). Essentially contested concepts. *Proceedings of the Aristotelian Society*, 56, 167–198.
Gamson, W. A. (1992). *Talking Politics*. Cambridge University Press.
Garre, M. (1999). *Human rights in translation: Legal concepts in different languages*. Copenhagen Business School Press.
Gattol, V., Sääksjärvi, M., Gill, T., & Schoormans, J. (2016). Feature fit: The role of congruence and complementarity when adding versus deleting features from products. *European Journal of Innovation Management*, 19(4), 589–607.
Gee, J. (2015). *Social linguistics and literacies: Ideology in discourses*. Fifth edition. Routledge.
Geeraerts, D. (2010). *Theories of lexical semantics*. Oxford University Press.
Geeraerts, D. (2006). Prototype theory: Problems and prospects of prototype theory. In D. Geeraerts (Ed.), *Cognitive linguistics: Basic readings* (pp. 141–165). De Gruyter Mouton.
Gennari, S. P., MacDonald, M. C., Postle, B. R., & Seidenberg, M. S. (2007). Context-dependent interpretation of words: Evidence for interactive neural processes. *Neuroimage*, 35(3), 1278–1286.
Ghidaoui, M. S., Zhao, M., McInnis, D. A., & Axworthy, D. H. (2005). A review of water hammer theory and practice. *Applied Mechanics Reviews*, 58(1), 49–76.

Giboreau, A., Dacremont, C., Egoroff, C., Guerrand, S., Urdapilleta, I., Candel, D., & Dubois, D. (2007). Defining sensory descriptors: Towards writing guidelines based on terminology. *Food Quality and Preference*, 18(2), 265–274.

Gidlöf, K., Wallin, A., Holmqvist, K., & Møgelvang-Hansen, P. (2013). Material distortion of economic behaviour and everyday decision quality. *Journal of Consumer Policy*, 36(4), 389–402.

Gill, T., & Dubé, L. (2007). What is a leather iron or a bird phone? Using conceptual combinations to generate and understand new product concepts. *Journal of Consumer Psychology*, 17(3), 202–217.

Giovagnoli, M. (2011). *Transmedia storytelling: Imagery, shapes and techniques*. ETC Press.

Gitlin, S. (2009). The meaning of 'Bing.' *New York Times*, June 7, 2009. URL: https://www.nytimes.com/2009/06/08/opinion/lweb08soft.html (accessed June 2020).

Glatter, R. (2014) Can smartphones adversely affect cognitive development in teens? *Forbes*. URL: https://www.forbes.com/sites/robertglatter/2014/05/19/can-smartphones-adversely-affect-cognitive-development-in-teens/#7976295c63bc (accessed June 20209).

Goffman, E. (1974). *Frame analysis: An essay on the organization of experience*. Harper and Row.

Goldberg, A. E. (2006). *Constructions at work: The nature of generalization in language*. Oxford University Press.

Graham, P. (2004). *Hackers and painters. Big ideas from the computer age*. O'Reilly Media.

Granata, G., Tartagilone, A. M., & Theodosios, T. (Eds.). (2019). *Predicting trends and building strategies for consumer engagement in retail environments*. IGI Global.

Graves, M. F., August, D., & Mancilla-Martinez, J. (2013). *Teaching vocabulary to English language learners*. Teachers College Press.

Grinyaev, S. (2001). Information warfare: The history, the present and the future. *Center for Strategic Assessment and Forecasts* (Russia). URL: http://csef.ru/en/politica-i-geopolitica/265/informaczionnaya-vojna-istoriya-den-segodnyashnij-i-perspektiva-538 (accessed June 2020).

Grist (2020). How to talk to a climate skeptic: Responses to the most common skeptical arguments on global warming. *Grist* 50. 2020. URL: https://grist.org/series/skeptics/ (accessed June 2020).

Groh, A. (2016). Culture, language and thought: Field studies on colour concepts. *Journal of Cognition and Culture*, 16(1–2), 83–106.

Grunig, J. E., & Hunt, T. (1984). *Managing public relations*. Thomson Learning.

Gumperz, J. J., & Levinson, S. C. (Eds.). (1996). *Rethinking linguistic relativity*. Cambridge University Press.

Hallahan, K. (1999). Seven models of framing: Implications for public relations. *Journal of Public Relations Research*, 11(3), 205–242.

References

Hammond, P. (2018). *Framing post-Cold War conflicts: The media and international intervention.* Manchester University Press.
Hampe, B., & Grady, J. E. (Eds.). (2005). *From perception to meaning: Image schemas in cognitive linguistics.* Vol. 29. De Gruyter Mouton.
Handl, S., & Schmid, H. (Eds.). (2011). *Windows to the mind: Metaphor, metonymy and conceptual blending.* De Gruyter Mouton.
Hardin, C. L., & Maffi, L., (Eds.). (1997). *Color categories in thought and language.* Cambridge University Press.
Harley, T. A. (2014). *The psychology of language: From data to theory.* Fourth edition. Psychology Press.
Harrell, L. (2014). 41 brand names people use as generic terms. *Mental Floss.* URL: http://mentalfloss.com/article/56667/41-brand-names-people-use-generic-terms (accessed June 2020).
Harris, A. (2014). Where I'm from: How a trip to Kenya changed the way I think about the terms African-American and black American. *Slate.* URL: https://slate.com/culture/2014/07/black-american-versus-african-american-why-i-prefer-to-be-called-a-black-american.html?via=gdpr-consent&via=gdpr-consent (accessed June 2020).
Heath, R. L., & Palenchar, M. J. (2008). *Strategic issues management: Organizations and public policy challenges.* Sage.
Herslund, M., & Baron, I. (2003). Language as world view: Endocentric and exocentric representations of reality. *Copenhagen Studies in Language*, 29, 29–42.
Herzog, R. J. (2007). A model of natural disaster administration: Naming and framing theory and reality. *Administrative Theory & Practice*, 29(4), 586–604.
Hilton, J. L., & von Hippel, W. (1996). Stereotypes. *Annual Review of Psychology*, 47(1), 237–271.
Hjelmslev, L. (1953 [1943]). *Prolegomena to a theory of language.* Translated by Francis J. Whitfield. Waverly Press.
Hobson, B., Lewis, J., & Siim, B. (Eds.). (2002). *Contested concepts in gender and social politics.* Edward Elgar Publishing.
Hockett, C. F. (1958). *A course in modern linguistics.* Macmillan.
Hoeffler, S. (2003) Measuring preferences for really new products. *Journal of Marketing Research*, 40(4), 406–420.
Hoeyer, K. (2005). Studying ethics as policy: The naming and framing of moral problems in genetic research. *Current Anthropology*, 46(S5), S71–S90.
Hollister, S. (2020). How fast are Apple's new ARM Mac chips? It's hard to tell. *The Verge.* June 23. URL: https://www.theverge.com/2020/6/23/21296365/apple-mac-arm-processor-silicon-chips-performance-power-speed-wwdc-2020 (accessed June 2020).
Holsanova, J. (2012). New methods for studying visual communication and multimodal integration. *Visual Communication* 11(3), 251–257.
Holsanova, J., Rahm, H., & Holmqvist, K. (2006). Entry points and reading paths on newspaper spreads: Comparing a semiotic analysis with eye-tracking measurements. *Visual Communication*, 5(1), 65–93.

Hörmann, H. (1986) *Meaning and context: An introduction to the psychology of language.* Plenum Press.

Hörmann, H. (1981). *To mean to understand: Problems of psychological semantics.* Springer.

Huh, Y. E., Vosgerau, J., & Morewedge, C. K. (2016). More similar but less satisfying: Comparing preferences for and the efficacy of within-and cross-category substitutes for food. *Psychological Science*, 27(6), 894–903.

Incardona, R., & Poncibò, C. (2007). The average consumer, the unfair commercial practices directive, and the cognitive revolution. *Journal of Consumer Policy*, 30(1), 21–38.

Irish, L. A., Kline, C. E., Gunn, H. E., Buysse, D. J., & Hall, M. H. (2015). The role of sleep hygiene in promoting public health: A review of empirical evidence. *Sleep Medicine Reviews*, 22, 23–36.

ISO (2009). *ISO 704. Terminology work: Principles and methods.* Third edition. Geneva: ISO.

Jackendoff, R. (1990). *Semantic structures.* MIT Press.

Jackson, C. A. (2016). Framing sex worker rights: How US sex worker rights activists perceive and respond to mainstream anti–sex trafficking advocacy. *Sociological Perspectives*, 59(1), 27–45.

Jakobson, R. (1959). On linguistic aspects of translation. In R. A. Bower (Ed.), *On translation* (pp. 232–239). Harvard University Press.

Jewitt, C., Bezemer, J. J., & O'Halloran, K. L. (2016). *Introducing multimodality.* Routledge.

Johnson-Laird, P. N. (2006). *How we reason.* Oxford University Press.

Jones, R. H. (2017). Discourse. In A. Barron, Y. Gu, & G. Steen (Eds.), *The Routledge handbook of pragmatics* (pp. 371–833). Routledge.

Jones, R. H. (2014). The multimodal dimension of claims in food packaging. *Multimodal Communication*, 3(1), 1–11.

Jowett, G. S., & O'Donnell, V. (2018). *Propaganda & persuasion.* Sage Publications.

Juhasz, B. J. (2018). Experience with compound words influences their processing: An eye movement investigation with English compound words. *The Quarterly Journal of Experimental Psychology*, 71(1), 103–112.

Kabel, L. (2017). *The coverage of Russia by the Danish media: On media created images and their consequences.* Nordic Council of Ministers & Ajour.

Kahneman, D. (2011). *Thinking, fast and slow.* Macmillan.

Kaufmann, H. R., Loureiro, S. M. C., & Manarioti, A. (2016). Exploring behavioural branding, brand love and brand co-creation. *Journal of Product & Brand Management*, 25(6), 516–526.

Keil, F. C., Stein, C., Webb, L., Billings, V. D., & Rozenblit, L. (2008). Discerning the division of cognitive labor: An emerging understanding of how knowledge is clustered in other minds. *Cognitive Science*, 32(2), 259–300.

Keller, K. L. (2016). Reflections on customer-based brand equity: Perspectives, progress, and priorities. *AMS Review*, 6(1–2), 1–16.

References

Keller, K. L. (2001). *Building customer-based brand equity: A blueprint for creating strong brands.* Marketing Science Institute.

Kellner, D. (2015). *Media spectacle and the crisis of democracy: Terrorism, war, and election battles.* Routledge.

Kennedy, G. A. (2008). *The art of rhetoric in the Roman world.* Wipf and Stock Publishers.

Kent, R. J., & Allen, C. T. (1994). Competitive interference effects in consumer memory for advertising: The role of brand familiarity. *Journal of Marketing,* 58(3), 97–105.

Kiefer, M., & Barsalou, L. W. (2013). Grounding the human conceptual system in perception, action, and internal states. In W. Prinz, M. Beisert, & A. Herwig (Eds.), *Action science: Foundations of an emerging discipline* (pp. 381–407). MIT Press.

Kim, J., Thomas, P., Sankaranarayana, R., Gedeon, T., & Yoon, H. J. (2015). Eye-tracking analysis of user behavior and performance in web search on large and small screens. *Journal of the Association for Information Science and Technology,* 66(3), 526–544.

Kim, S., Suh, E., & Hwang, H. (2003). Building the knowledge map: An industrial case study. *Journal of Knowledge Management,* 7(2), 34–45.

Kittay, E., & Lehrer, A. (Eds.). (1992). *Frames, fields, and contrasts: New essays in semantic and lexical organization.* Lawrence Erlbaum Associates.

Klein, H. (2018). Information warfare and information operations: Russian and U.S. perspectives. *Journal of International Affairs,* 71 (Special Issue), 135–142.

Klimchuk, M. R., & Krasovec, S. A. (2013). *Packaging design: Successful product branding from concept to shelf.* John Wiley & Sons.

Klink, R. R. (2001). Creating meaningful new brand names: A study of semantics and sound symbolism. *Journal of Marketing Theory and Practice,* 9(2), 27–34.

Klüver, H., & Sagarzazu, I. (2016). Setting the agenda or responding to voters? Political parties, voters and issue attention. *West European Politics,* 39(2), 380–398.

Knüpfer, C. B., & Entman, R. M. (2018). Framing conflicts in digital and transnational media environments. *Media, War & Conflict,* 11(4), 476–488.

Kockaert, H. J., & Steurs, F. (Eds.). (2015). *Handbook of terminology.* John Benjamins.

Kohli, C., & LaBahn, D. W. (1997). Creating effective brand names: A study of the naming process. *Journal of Advertising Research,* 37(1), 67–75.

Kone, A. M. (2013). Between linguistic universalism and linguistic relativism: Perspectives on human understandings of reality. *Inquiries,* 5(9). URL: http://www.inquiriesjournal.com/a?id=761 (accessed June 2020).

Korzen, I. (2016). Endocentric and exocentric verb typology: Talmy revisited – on good grounds. *Language and Cognition,* 8(2), 206–236.

Korzen, I. (2006). Endocentric and exocentric languages in translation. *Perspectives: Studies in Translatology,* 13(1): 21–37.

Koster, D., & Cadierno, T. (2018). Is perception of placement universal? A mixed methods perspective on linguistic relativity. *Lingua*, 207, 23–37.

Kress, G. (2010) *Multimodality. A social semiotic approach to contemporary communication*. Routledge.

Kress, G. (1993). Against arbitrariness: The social production of the sign as a foundational issue in critical discourse analysis. *Discourse & Society*, 4(2), 169–191.

Kress, G., & van Leeuwen, T. V. (2001). *Multimodal discourse: The modes and media of contemporary communication*. Hodder Education.

Krishna, A. (2012). An integrative review of sensory marketing: Engaging the senses to affect perception, judgment and behavior. *Journal of Consumer Psychology*, 22(3), 332–351.

Krott, A. (2009). The role of analogy for compound words. In J. P. Blevins & J. Blevins (Eds.), *Analogy in grammar: Form and acquisition* (pp. 118–136). Oxford University Press.

Krott, A., & Nicoladis, E. (2005). Large constituent families help children parse compounds. *Journal of Child Language*, 32(1), 139–158.

Kumar, D. (2006). Media, war, and propaganda: Strategies of information management during the 2003 Iraq war. *Communication and Critical/Cultural Studies*, 3(1), 48–69.

Kurtz, K. J., & Gentner, D. (2001). Kinds of kinds: Sources of category coherence. In J. D. Moore & K. Stenning (Eds.), *Proceedings of the Annual Meeting of the Cognitive Science Society* (pp. 522–527). Lawrence Erlbaum Associates.

Lähteenmäki, L., Lampila, P., Grunert, K., Boztug, Y., Ueland, Ø., Åström, A., & Martinsdóttir, E. (2010). Impact of health-related claims on the perception of other product attributes. *Food Policy*, 35(3), 230–239.

Lakoff, G. (1987). *Women, fire, and dangerous things. What categories reveal about the mind*. University of Chicago Press.

Langacker, R. W. (1987). *Foundations of cognitive grammar: Theoretical prerequisites*. Vol. 1. Stanford University Press.

LaPlante-Dube, S. (2017). How to market services – treat them like a product. *Precision Marketing Group*. URL: https://www.precisionmarketinggroup.com/blog/bid/76722/how-to-market-services-treat-them-like-a-product (accessed June 2020).

Leape, J. (2006). The London congestion charge. *Journal of Economic Perspectives*, 20(4), 157–176.

Lecheler, S., Bos, L., & Vliegenthart, R. (2015). The mediating role of emotions: News framing effects on opinions about immigration. *Journalism & Mass Communication Quarterly*, 92(4), 812–838.

Ledin, P., & Machin, D. (2020). *Introduction to multimodal analysis*. Bloomsbury Publishing.

Ledingham, J. A. (2003). Explicating relationship management as a general theory of public relations. *Journal of Public Relations Research*, 15(2), 181–198.

Lee, Y. H., & Ang, K. S. (2003). Brand name suggestiveness: A Chinese language perspective. *International Journal of Research in Marketing*, 20(4), 323–335.

Legrand, P. (1997a). Against a European civil code. *The Modern Law Review*, 60(1), 44–63.

Legrand, P. (1997b). The impossibility of "legal transplants." *Maastricht Journal of European and Comparative Law*, 4(2), 111–124.

Leopold, W. (1929). Inner form. *Language*, 5(4), 254–260.

Levy, J., & Jakobsson, P. (2014). Sweden's abolitionist discourse and law: Effects on the dynamics of Swedish sex work and on the lives of Sweden's sex workers. *Criminology & Criminal Justice*, 14(5), 593–607.

Libben, G. (2014). The nature of compounds: A psychocentric perspective. *Cognitive Neuropsychology*, 31(1–2), 8–25.

Libben, G., & Jarema, G. (Eds.). (2006). *The representation and processing of compound words*. Oxford University Press.

Liu, B., Chin, C. W., & Ng, H. T. (2003). Mining topic-specific concepts and definitions on the web. In *Proceedings of the 12th international conference on World Wide Web* (pp. 251–260). ACM.

Loftus, E. F., & Palmer, J. C. (1974). Reconstruction of automobile destruction: An example of the interaction between language and memory. *Journal of Verbal Learning and Verbal Behavior*, 13(5), 585–589.

Luntz, F. (2007). *Words that work: It's not what you say, it's what people hear*. Hyperion.

Lynch, J. A., & Zoller, H. (2015). Recognizing differences and commonalities: The rhetoric of health and medicine and critical-interpretive health communication. *Communication Quarterly*, 63(5), 498–503.

Lynott, D., & Connell, L. (2010). Embodied conceptual combination. *Frontiers in Psychology*, 1, 212. URL: https://doi.org/10.3389/fpsyg.2010.00212 (accesses June 2020).

Lyons, J. (1977). *Semantics*. Vol. 1–2. Cambridge University Press.

MacMaoláin, C. (2015). *Food law: European, domestic and international frameworks*. Bloomsbury Publishing.

MacMaoláin, C. (2007). *EU food law: Protecting consumers and health in a common market*. Bloomsbury Publishing.

Macnamara, J., Lwin, M., Adi, A., & Zerfass, A. (2016). 'PESO' media strategy shifts to 'SOEP': Opportunities and ethical dilemmas. *Public Relations Review*, 42(3), 377–385.

Madsen, B. M., & Thomsen, H. E. (2015). Concept modelling vs. data modelling in practice. In H. J. Kockaert & F. Steurs (Eds.), *Handbook of terminology* (pp. 250–275). John Benjamins.

Malt, B. C., Gennari, S., & Imai, M. (2010). Lexicalization patterns and the world-to-words mapping. In B. C. Malt and P. Wolff (Eds.), *Words and the mind: How words capture human experience* (pp. 29–57). Oxford University Press.

Malt, B. C., & Wolff, P. (Eds.). (2010). *Words and the mind: How words capture human experience*. Oxford University Press.

Manelis, L., & Tharp, D. A. (1977). The processing of affixed words. *Memory & Cognition*, 5(6), 690–695.

Marius, B. (2016), The journey to discover the true meaning of a startup. *Bmarius.com*. URL: https://bmarius.com/a-journey-to-discover-the-true-meaning-of-a-startup-21bb20b1dfd6 (accessed June 2020).

Markman, E. M. (1990). Constraints children place on word meanings. *Cognitive Science*, 14(1), 57–77.

Martin, J. R., & White, P. R. R. (2003). *The language of evaluation: Appraisal in English.* Palgrave Macmillan.

Marzo, D. (2015). Motivation, compositionality, idiomatization. In P. O. Müller, I. Ohnheiser, S. Olsen, & F. Rainer (Eds.), *Word formation. An international handbook of the languages of Europe.* Vol. 1–2 (pp. 984–1001). De Gruyter Mouton.

Mathews, D. (2016). *Naming and framing difficult issues to make sound decisions.* Kettering Foundation.

Matthews, J. (2009). What's in a frame? A content analysis of media-framing studies in the world's leading communication journals, 1990–2005. *Journalism & Mass Communication Quarterly*, 86(2), 349–367.

Maurya, U. K., & Mishra, P. (2012). What is a brand? A perspective on brand meaning. *European Journal of Business and Management*, 4(3), 122–133.

Mautner, G. (2016). *Discourse and management: Critical perspectives through the language lens.* Macmillan.

McCombs, M. (1997). New frontiers in agenda setting: Agendas of attributes and frames. *Mass Communication Review*, 24(1&2), 32–52.

McCroskey, J. C. (2016). *An Introduction to rhetorical communication.* Ninth edition. Routledge.

McWhorter, J. (2003). *The power of babel: A natural history of language.* Random House.

Meijers, M. H., Remmelswaal, P., & Wonneberger, A. (2018). Using visual impact metaphors to stimulate environmentally friendly behavior: The roles of response efficacy and evaluative persuasion knowledge. *Environmental Communication*, 1–14. DOI: 10.1080/17524032.2018.1544160

Messaris, P. (2012). Visual "literacy" in the digital age. *Review of Communication*, 12(2), 101–117.

Messaris, P. (1997). *Visual persuasion: The role of images in advertising.* Sage.

Mey, J. L. (1985). *Whose language? A Study in linguistic pragmatics.* John Benjamins.

Miller, D., & Dinan, W. (2008). *A century of spin: How public relations became the cutting edge of corporate power.* Pluto Press.

Møgelvang-Hansen, P. (2010). Misleading presentation of food: Methods of legal regulation and real-life case scenarios. In H. W. Micklitz, V. Smith, & M. Ohm Rørdam (Eds.), *New challenges for the assessment of fairness in a common market.* EUI Working Papers LAW, 21 (pp. 49–57). European University Institute.

Molander, R. C., Riddile, A., Wilson, P. A., & Williamson, S. (1996). *Strategic information warfare: A new face of war.* RAND.

Mori, Y., & Nagy, W. (1999). Integration of information from context and word elements in interpreting novel kanji compounds. *Reading Research Quarterly*, 34(1), 80–101.

Moskowitz, H. R., Reisner, M., Itty, B., Katz, R., & Krieger, B. (2006). Steps towards a consumer-driven 'concept innovation machine' for food and drink. *Food Quality and Preference*, 17(7–8), 536–551.

Müller, P. O., Ohnheiser, I., Olsen, S., & Rainer, F. (Eds.). (2015). *Word formation. An International handbook of the languages of Europe.* Vol. 1–2. De Gruyter Mouton.

Mulligan, K. (Ed.). (1990). *Mind, meaning and metaphysics: The philosophy and theory of language of Anton Marty.* Springer.

Murphy, G. L. (2010). What are categories and concepts? In D. Mareschall, P. C. Quin, & S. E. G. Lea (Eds.), *The making of human concepts* (pp. 11–28). Oxford University Press.

Murphy, G. L. (2004). *The big book of concepts.* MIT Press.

Murphy, J. (1992). What is branding? In J. Murphy (Ed.), *Branding, a key marketing tool* (pp. 1–12). Macmillan.

Muzellec, L. (2006). What is in a name change? Re-joycing corporate names to create corporate brands. *Corporate Reputation Review*, 8(4), 305–316.

Nagy, W. E. (1995). *On the role of context in first-and second-language vocabulary learning.* University of Illinois.

NCI. (2019). Cell phones and cancer risk. *National Cancer Institute.* URL: https://www.cancer.gov/about-cancer/causes-prevention/risk/radiation/cell-phones-fact-sheet?redirect=true (accessed June 2020).

Nelson, T. E., Oxley, Z. M., & Clawson, R. A. (1997). Towards a psychology of framing effects. *Political Behavior*, 19(3), 221–246.

Newen, A., & Bartels, A. (2007). Animal minds and the possession of concepts. *Philosophical Psychology*, 20(3), 283–308.

Nguyen, S. P., & McCullough, M. B. (2009). Making sense of what is healthy for you: Children and adults evaluative categories of food. In S. J. Ellsworth & R. C. Schuster (Eds.), *Appetite and Nutritional Assessment* (pp. 175–187). Nova Science Publishers.

Nguyen, T. T., Hui, P. M., Harper, F. M., Terveen, L., & Konstan, J. A. (2014). Exploring the filter bubble: The effect of using recommender systems on content diversity. In *Proceedings of the 23rd international conference on world wide web* (pp. 677–686). ACM.

Nielsen, J. H., Escalas, J. E., & Hoeffler, S. (2018). Mental simulation and category knowledge affect really new product evaluation through transportation. *Journal of Experimental Psychology: Applied*, 24(2), 145–158.

Nisbett, R. E., & Wilson, T. D. (1977). The halo effect: Evidence for unconscious alteration of judgments. *Journal of Personality and Social Psychology*, 35(4), 250–256.

Nöth, W. (1995). *Handbook of semiotics.* Indiana University Press.

O'Brien, K., Eriksen, S., Nygaard, L. P., & Schjolden, A. N. E. (2007). Why different interpretations of vulnerability matter in climate change discourses. *Climate Policy*, 7(1), 73–88.

OED (2018). New words list, January 2018. *Oxford English Dictionary (OED)*. URL: https://public.oed.com/updates/new-words-list-january-2018/ (accessed June 2020).

O'Halloran, K. L., Tan, S., & Marissa, K. L. E. (2017). Multimodal analysis for critical thinking. *Learning, Media and Technology*, 42(2), 147–170.

O'Halloran, K. L., Tan, S., Pham, D. S., Bateman, J., & Vande Moere, A. (2018). A digital mixed methods research design: Integrating multimodal analysis with data mining and information visualization for big data analytics. *Journal of Mixed Methods Research*, 12(1), 11–30.

Ojala, M. M., Pantti, M. K., & Kangas, J. (2017). Whose war, whose fault? Visual framing of the Ukraine conflict in Western European newspapers. *International Journal of Communication*, 11, 474–498.

O'Keefe, D. J. (2016). *Persuasion: Theory and research*. Third edition. Sage.

Ooms, K., Coltekin, A., De Maeyer, P., Dupont, L., Fabrikant, S., Incoul, A., ... & Van der Haegen, L. (2015). Combining user logging with eye tracking for interactive and dynamic applications. *Behavior Research Methods*, 47(4), 977–993.

Orquin, J. L., & Loose, S. M. (2013). Attention and choice: A review on eye movements in decision making. *Acta Psychologica*, 144(1), 190–206.

Özcan, E., & van Egmond, R. (2012). Basic semantics of product sounds. *International Journal of Design*, 6(2), 41–54.

Painter, N. I. (2006). *Creating black Americans: African-American history and its meanings, 1619 to the present*. Oxford University Press.

Papafragou, A., Massey, C., & Gleitman, L. (2002). Shake, rattle, 'n' roll: The representation of motion in language and cognition. *Cognition*, 84(2), 189–219.

Paradis, C. (2004). Where does metonymy stop? Senses, facets, and active zones. *Metaphor and Symbol*, 19(4), 245–264.

Pariser, E. (2011). *The filter bubble: What the Internet is hiding from you*. Penguin.

Park, C. (2014). Naming and framing. *Art of Simple*. Blog founded by Tsh Oxenreider. URL: https://theartofsimple.net/naming-and-framing/ (accessed June 2020).

Park, Y., & Chen, J. V. (2007). Acceptance and adoption of the innovative use of smartphone. *Industrial Management & Data Systems*, 107(9), 1349–1365.

Patterson, K., Nestor, P. J., & Rogers, T. T. (2007). Where do you know what you know? The representation of semantic knowledge in the human brain. *Nature Reviews Neuroscience*, 8, 976–987.

Pavlenko, A. (2014). *The bilingual mind and what it tells us about language and thought*. Cambridge University Press.

Pessin, A., & Goldberg, S. (Eds.). (1996). *The Twin Earth chronicles: Twenty years of reflection on Hilary Putnam's the "Meaning of Meaning."* Routledge.

Peterson, R. D., & Palmer, C. L. (2017). Effects of physical attractiveness on political beliefs. *Politics and the Life Sciences*, 36(2), 3–16.

Petty, R. E., & Cacioppo, J. T. (1986). *Communication and persuasion: Central and peripheral routes to attitude change*. Springer.

Piaget, J. (2002 [1926]). *The language and thought of the child*. Third edition. Routledge.

Pieters, R., & Warlop, L. (1999). Visual attention during brand choice: The impact of time pressure and task motivation. *International Journal of research in Marketing*, 16(1), 1–16.

Pinker, S. (1994). *The language instinct: The new science of language and mind*. Penguin.

Pinto, H. S., & Martins, J, P. (2004). Ontologies: How can They be Built? *Knowledge and Information Systems*, 6, 441–464.

Pinxten, R. (Ed.) (1976). *Universalism versus relativism in language and thought*. Mouton.

Poberezhskaya, M., & Ashe, T. (Eds.). (2018). *Climate change discourse in Russia: Past and present*. Routledge.

Pollack, K. M. (2004). Spies, lies, and weapons: What went wrong. *The Atlantic Monthly*, 293(1), 78–92.

Powell, T. E. (2017). *Multimodal news framing effects*. PhD Thesis. University of Amsterdam.

Powell, T. E., Boomgaarden, H. G., de Swert, K., & de Vreese, C. H. (2019). Framing fast and slow: A dual processing account of multimodal framing effects. *Media Psychology*, 22(4), 572–600.

Powell, T. E., Boomgaarden, H. G., de Swert, K., & de Vreese, C. H. (2015). A clearer picture: The contribution of visuals and text to framing effects. *Journal of Communication*, 65(6), 997–1017.

Prince, P. (1996). Second language vocabulary learning: The role of context versus translations as a function of proficiency. *The Modern Language Journal*, 80(4), 478–493.

PRSA. (2018). PRSA Code of Ethics. *Public Relations Society of America*. URL: https://www.prsa.org/ethics/code-of-ethics (accessed June 2020).

Putnam, H. (1975a). The meaning of 'meaning'. In H. Putnam (Ed.), *Mind, Language and Reality. Philosophical Papers*. Vol. 2 (pp. 215–271). Cambridge University Press.

Putnam, H. (1975b). Is semantics possible? In H. Putnam (Ed.), *Mind, Language and Reality. Philosophical Papers*. Vol. 2 (pp. 139–152). Cambridge University Press.

Ramscar, M. J., & Port, R. (2015). Categorization (without categories). In E. Dabrowska & D. Divjak (Eds.), *Handbook of cognitive linguistics* (pp. 75–99). De Gruyter Mouton.

Ran, B., & Duimering, P. R. (2010). Conceptual combination: Models, theories and controversies. *International Journal of Cognitive Linguistics*, 1(1), 65–90.

Ratneshwar, S., Barsalou, L.W., Pechmann, C., & Moore, M. (2001). Goal derived categories: The role of personal and situational goals in category representation. *Journal of Consumer Psychology*, 10(3), 147–157.

Rebollar, R., Lidón, I., Martín, J., & Puebla, M. (2015). The identification of viewing patterns of chocolate snack packages using eye-tracking techniques. *Food Quality and Preference*, 39, 251–258.

Reese, S. D. (2010). Finding frames in the web of culture: The case of the war on terror. In O. D'Angelo & J. A. Kuypers (Eds.), *Doing news framing analysis* (pp. 33–58). Routledge.

Regier, T., Kay, P., Gilbert, A. L., & Ivry, R. B. (2010). Language and thought: Which side are you on, anyway? In B. C. Malt & P. Wolff (Eds.), *Words and the Mind: How words capture human experience* (pp. 165–182). Oxford University Press.

Resnick, P., Garrett, R. K., Kriplean, T., Munson, S. A., & Stroud, N. J. (2013). Bursting your (filter) bubble: Strategies for promoting diverse exposure. In *Proceedings of the 2013 conference on Computer supported cooperative work companion* (pp. 95–100). The ACM Digital Library.

Ribeiro, F., & Cerveira, M. E. (Eds.). (2018). *Challenges and opportunities for knowledge organization in the digital age*. Ergon.

Rideout, B. (2008). Storytelling, narrative rationality, and legal persuasion. *The Journal of the Legal Writing Institute*, 14, 53–86.

Ries, E. (2011). *The lean startup*. Crown Business.

Riezebos, R., Kist, B., & Kootstra, G. (2003). *Brand management: A theoretical and practical approach*. Prentice Hall.

Rindell, A. (2008). *What brands mean to us: A short introduction to brand research within Consumer Culture Theory*. HAAGA-HELIA Publications.

Roberts-Miller, P. (2002). Post-contemporary composition: Social constructivism and its alternatives. *Composition Studies*, 30(1), 97–116.

Rodin, M. (1992). The social construction of premenstrual syndrome. *Social Science & Medicine*, 35(1), 49–56.

Roe, B. E., Levy, A. S., & Derby, B. M. (1999). The impact of health claims on consumer search and product evaluation outcomes: Results from FDA experimental data. *Journal of Public Policy and Marketing*, 18(1), 89–115

Rogers, E. M. (2010). *Diffusion of innovations*. Fourth edition. The Free Press.

Rojo, A., & Cifuentes-Férez, P. (2017). On the reception of translations: Exploring the impact of typological differences on legal contexts. In I. Ibarretxe-Antuñano (Ed.), *Motion and Space across Languages* (pp. 367–398). John Benjamins.

Rosch, E. (1975). Cognitive representations of semantic categories. *Journal of Experimental Psychology: General*, 104(3), 192–233.

Ross, B. H., & Murphy, G. L. (1999). Food for thought: Cross-classification and category organization in a complex real-world domain. *Cognitive Psychology*, 38(4), 495–553.

Rumelhart, D. (1980). Schemata: The building blocks of cognition. In R. Spiro, B. Bruce, & W. Brewer (Eds.), *Theoretical issues in reading comprehension* (pp. 33–58). Lawrence Erlbaum.

Rundh, B. (2009). Packaging design: Creating competitive advantage with product packaging. *British Food Journal*, 111(9), 988–1002.

Ryder, M. E. (1994). *Ordered chaos: The interpretation of English noun-noun compounds.* University of California Press.

Sager, J. C. (1990). *Practical course in terminology processing.* John Benjamins.

SALC. (2019). What is SALC? *The Scandinavian Association for Language and Cognition.* URL: http://www.salc-sssk.org/home/what-is-salc// (accessed June 2020).

Sandra, D. (1990). On the representation and processing of compound words: Automatic access to constituent morphemes does not occur. *Quarterly Journal of Experimental Psychology*, 42A, 529–567.

Schäfer, M. (2018). *The semantic transparency of English compound nouns.* Language Science Press.

Schaffner, B. F., & Sellers, P. J. (2010). *Winning with words: The origins and impact of political framing.* Routledge.

Schank, R. C. (1999). *Dynamic memory revisited.* Cambridge University Press.

Scherer, K. R., Schorr, A., & Johnstone, T. (Eds.). (2001). *Appraisal processes in emotion: Theory, methods, research.* Oxford University Press.

Scheufele, D. A. (1999). Framing as a theory of media effects. *Journal of Communication*, 49(1), 103–122.

Schmid, H. J. (2011). Conceptual blending, relevance and novel N+N-compounds. In S. Handl and H. J. Schmid (Eds.), *Windows to the mind: Metaphor, metonymy and conceptual blending* (pp. 219–245). De Gruyter Mouton.

Schmidtke, D., Matsuki, K., & Kuperman, V. (2017). Surviving blind decomposition: A distributional analysis of the time-course of complex word recognition. *Journal of Experimental Psychology: Learning, Memory, and Cognition*, 43(11), 1793–1820.

Schwartz, B. (2004). *The paradox of choice: Why more is less.* Ecco.

Shah, J. (2018). How to generate name ideas for political movements. *Design-Hill.* October 26, 2018. URL: https://www.designhill.com/design-blog/how-to-generate-name-ideas-for-political-parties/ (accessed June 2020).

Shahab, L., Goniewicz, M. L., Blount, B. C., Brown, J., McNeill, A., Alwis, K. U., ... & West, R. (2017). Nicotine, carcinogen, and toxin exposure in long-term e-cigarette and nicotine replacement therapy users: A cross-sectional study. *Annals of Internal Medicine*, 166(6), 390–400.

Shakespeare, W. (2010 [1597]). *Romeo and Juliet.* Edited by J. O'Connor. Longman.

Shocker, A. D., Bayus, B. L., & Kim, N. (2004). Product complements and substitutes in the real world: The relevance of "other products." *Journal of Marketing*, 68(1), 28–40.

Shrum, L. J., & Lowrey, T. M. (2007). Sounds convey meaning: The Implications of phonetic symbolism for brand name construction. In T. M. Lowrey (Ed.), *Psycholinguistic phenomena in marketing communications* (pp. 39–58). Lawrence Erlbaum Associates.

Sidhu, D. M., & Pexman, P. M. (2018). Five mechanisms of sound symbolic association. *Psychonomic Bulletin & Review*, 25(5), 1619–1643.

Simard, D. (2004). Using diaries to promote metalinguistic reflection among elementary school students. *Language Awareness*, 13(1), 34–48.

Simmons, W. K., Martin, A., & Barsalou, L. W. (2005). Pictures of appetizing foods activate gustatory cortices for taste and reward. *Cerebral Cortex*, 15(10), 1602–1608.

Simonet, P. (2016). How the best marketing channel is the packaging. *Media Marketing*. URL: https://www.media-marketing.com/en/opinion/how-the-best-marketing-channel-is-the-packaging (accessed June 2020).

Singh, P., Barry, B., & Liu, H. (2004). Teaching machines about everyday life. *BT Technology Journal*, 22(4), 227–240.

Slobin, D. I. (2004). The many ways to search for a frog: Linguistic typology and the expression of motion events. In S. Strömqvist & L. Verhoeven (Eds.), *Relating events in narrative: Typological and contextual perspectives* (pp. 219–257). Lawrence Erlbaum Associates.

Slobin, D. I. (1996). From 'thought and language' to 'thinking for speaking'. In J. Gumperz & S. Levinson (Eds.), *Rethinking linguistic relativity* (pp. 70–96). Cambridge University Press.

Smith, J. (2017). *The UK's Journeys into and out of the EU: Destinations Unknown*. Routledge.

Smith, A. N., Fischer, E., & Yongjian, C. (2012). How does brand-related user-generated content differ across YouTube, Facebook, and Twitter? *Journal of Interactive Marketing*, 26(2), 102–113.

Smith, E. E., Shoben, E. J., & Rips, L. J. (1974). Structure and process in semantic memory: A featural model for semantic decisions. *Psychological Review*, 81(3), 214–241.

Smith, J., Zakrzewski, A., Johnson, J., Valleau, J., & Church, B. (2016). Categorization: The view from animal cognition. *Behavioral Sciences*, 6(2), 12.

Smith, V. (2000). On the contrastive study of lexicalization patterns for translation purposes: Some reflections on the levels of analysis. In I. Korzen & C. Marello (Eds.), *On linguistic aspects of translation* (pp. 19–42). Edizione dell'Orso.

Smith, V., Barratt, D., & Sørensen, H. S. (2015). Do natural pictures mean natural tastes? Assessing visual semantics experimentally. *Cognitive Semiotics*, 8(1), 53–86.

Smith, V., Barratt, D., & Zlatev, J. (2014). Unpacking noun-noun compounds: Interpreting novel and conventional food names in isolation and on food labels. *Cognitive Linguistics*, 25(1), 99–147.

Smith, V., Clement, J., Møgelvang-Hansen, P., & Selsøe Sørensen, H. (2011). Assessing in-store food-to-consumer communication from a fairness

perspective: An integrated approach. *Fachsprache – International Journal of Specialized Communication*, 33(1–2), 84–106.
Smith, V., Green-Petersen, D., Møgelvang-Hansen, P., Christensen, R. H. B., Qvistgaard, F, & Hyldig, G. (2013). What's (in) a real smoothie: A division of linguistic labour in consumers' acceptance of name-product combinations? *Appetite*, 63, 129–140.
Smith, V., Ohm Søndergaard, M., Clement, J., Møgelvang-Hansen, P., Selsøe Sørensen, H., & Gabrielsen, G. (2009). *Fair Speak: Scenarier for vildledning på det danske fødevaremarked*. [Fair speak: Scenarios of misleading practices on the Danish food market.] ExTuto.
Smith, V., Møgelvang-Hansen, P., & Hyldig, G. (2010). Spin versus fair speak in food labelling: A matter of taste? *Food Quality and Preference*, 21(8), 1016–1025.
Sojka, J. Z., & Giese, J. L. (2006). Communicating through pictures and words: Understanding the role of affect and cognition in processing visual and verbal information. *Psychology & Marketing*, 23(12), 995–1014.
Sommers-Flanagan, J., & Sommers-Flanagan, R. (2018). *Counseling and psychotherapy theories in context and practice: Skills, strategies, and techniques*. John Wiley & Sons.
Song, M. X., & Montoya-Weiss, M. M. (1998). Critical development activities for really new versus incremental products. *Journal of Product Innovation Management*, 15(2), 124–135.
Sperber, D., & Wilson, D. (1995). *Relevance: Communication and cognition*. Second edition. Blackwell.
Štekauer, P. (2005). *Meaning predictability in word formation*. John Benjamins.
Stepanski, E. J., & Wyatt, J. K. (2003). Use of sleep hygiene in the treatment of insomnia. *Sleep Medicine Reviews*, 7(3), 215–225.
Susarla, A., Oh, J. H., & Tan, Y. (2012). Social networks and the diffusion of user-generated content: Evidence from YouTube. *Information Systems Research*, 23(1), 23–41.
Swaminathan, V., Gürhan-Canli, Z., Kubat, U., & Hayran, C. (2015). How, when, and why do attribute-complementary versus attribute-similar cobrands affect brand evaluations: A concept combination perspective. *Journal of Consumer Research*, 42(1), 45–58.
Tabansky, L. (2017). Cybered influence operations: Towards a scientific research agenda. *The Norwegian Atlantic Committee. Security Policy Library*, 2, 1–36.
Tabansky, L. (2013). Does cyberspace promote human rights and democracy?: Applying Karl Popper's scientific method. *The International Journal of Science in Society*, 4(4), 13–23.
Taillard, M. O. (2000). Persuasive communication: The case of marketing. *Working Papers in Linguistics*, 12, 145–174.
Talmy, L. (2000). *Toward a cognitive semantics. Volume II: Typology and process in concept structuring*. MIT Press.

Tannen, D. E. (1993). *Framing in discourse*. Oxford University Press.
Ten Hacken, P., & Panocová, R. (Eds.). (2015). *Word formation and transparency in medical English*. Cambridge Scholars Publishing.
The Language Nerds. (2019). Product names that mean something unfortunate in other languages. *The Language Nerds*. URL: http://thelanguagenerds.com/product-names-that-mean-something-unfortunate-in-other-languages/ (accessed January 2020).
Thomas, R. (1992). *Literacy and orality in ancient Greece*. Cambridge University Press.
Thomas, T. (2015). Russia's 21st century information war: Working to undermine and destabilize populations. *Defense Strategic Communications*, 1(2), 11–26.
Thomson, D. M. H., & Crocker, C. (2015). Application of conceptual profiling in brand, packaging and product development. *Food Quality and Preference*, 40(Part B), 343–353.
Tomasello, M. (2003). *Constructing a language*. Harvard University Press.
Trzaskowski, J. (2011). Behavioural economics, neuroscience, and the Unfair Commercial Practises Directive. *Journal of Consumer Policy*, 34(3), 377.
Tse, C. S., & Altarriba, J. (2008). Evidence against linguistic relativity in Chinese and English: A case study of spatial and temporal metaphors. *Journal of Cognition and Culture*, 8(3–4), 335–357.
UCPD. (2005). *Directive 2005/29/EC of the European Parliament and of the Council of 11 May 2005 concerning unfair business-to-consumer commercial practices in the internal market*. URL: https://eur-lex.europa.eu/legal-content/EN/TXT/?uri=CELEX%3A32005L0029 (accessed June 2020).
Ullmann, S. (1962). *Semantics: An introduction to the science of meaning*. Blackwell.
Usunier, J. C., & Shaner, J. (2002). Using linguistics for creating better international brand names. *Journal of Marketing Communications*, 8(4), 211–228.
Vermeulen, N., Corneille, O., & Niedenthal, P. M. (2008). Sensory load incurs conceptual processing costs. *Cognition*, 109(2), 287–294.
Verschueren, J. (1998). *Understanding pragmatics*. Oxford University Press.
Vliegenthart, R., & van Zoonen, L. (2011) Power to the frame: Bringing sociology back to frame analysis. *European Journal of Communication*, 26(2), 101–115.
von Humboldt, W. (1999 [1836]). On language: On the diversity of human language construction and its influence on the mental development of the human species. Edited by Michael Losonsky. Cambridge University Press.
Vygotsky, L. S. (2012 [1934]). *Thought and language*. MIT press.
Walker, F. (n.d.) 15 of the worst car names ever. *DriveTribe*. URL: https://drivetribe.com/p/15-of-the-worst-car-names-ever-Uuj3c_VxR7aCu-WkDCeahg?iid=d6iUMcm-Qp2E_pbcirK9Jw (accessed June 2020).

Walsh, J. (2017). We were lied to: Voters who have changed their mind on Brexit. *The Guardian*. Wednesday October 17. URL: https://www.theguardian.com/politics/2017/oct/11/we-were-lied-to-voters-who-have-changed-their-mind-on-brexit (accessed June 2020).

Wansink, B., & Chandon, P. (2006). Can 'low-fat' nutrition labels lead to obesity? *Journal of Marketing Research*, 43(4), 605–617.

Waugh, L. R. (1993). Against arbitrariness: Imitation and motivation revived, with consequences for textual meaning. *Diacritics*, 23(2), 71–87.

Webster, F. (2014). *Theories of the information society*. Fourth edition. Routledge.

Western States Center. (2003). Dismantling racism: A resource book for social change groups. *Western States Center*. Portland, OR: URL: http://westernstates.center/tools-and-resources/Tools/Dismantling%20Racism (accessed June 2020).

Whorf, B. L. (1956) *Language, thought, and reality: Selected writings of Benjamin Lee Whorf*. Edited by John B. Carroll. MIT Press.

Widdowson, H. G. (1995). Discourse analysis: A critical view. *Language and Literature*, 4(3), 157–172.

Wierzbicka, A. (1997). *Understanding cultures through their key words: English, Russian, Polish, German, and Japanese*. Oxford University Press.

Wierzbicka, A. (1985). *Lexicography and conceptual analysis*. Ann Arbor: Karoma.

Williams, J. N. (1992). Processing polysemous words in context: Evidence for interrelated meanings. *Journal of Psycholinguistic Research*, 21(3), 193–218.

Willis, J. (1981). *Teaching English through English*. Longman.

Wilson, D., & Carston, R. (2007). A unitary approach to lexical pragmatics: Relevance, inference and ad hoc concepts. In N. Burton-Roberts (Ed.), *Pragmatics* (pp. 230–260). Palgrave-Macmillan.

Wilson, D., & Sperber, D. (2012). *Meaning and relevance*. Cambridge University Press.

Wintour, P., MacAskill, E., Borger, J., & Chrisafis, A. (2018). US says it has proof Assad's regime carried out Douma gas attack. *The Guardian*. April 13, 2018. URL: https://www.theguardian.com/world/2018/apr/13/uk-denounces-claims-it-was-behind-staged-syrian-gas-attack (accessed June 2020).

Wisniewski, E. J. (1996). Construal and similarity in conceptual combination. *Journal of Memory and Language*, 35(3), 434–453.

Wood, M. L. (1991). Naming the illness: The power of words. *Family Medicine*, 23(7), 534–538.

Wozniak, S. (2006). *iWoz: Computer geek to cult icon*. W.W. Norton & Company.

Wright, S. E., & Budin, G. (Eds.). (1997). *Handbook of terminology management*. Vol. 1. John Benjamins.

Wüster, E. (1959/1960). Das Worten der Welt: Schaubildlich und terminologisch dargestellt. [The wording of the world: Schematically and terminologically reproduced.] *Sprachforum*, 3/4, 183–203.

Wyer, Jr, R. S., & Srull, T. K. (2014). *Memory and cognition in its social context*. Psychology Press.
Yates, K., Friedman, K., Slater, M. D., Berman, M., Paskett, E., & Ferketich, A. K. (2015). A content analysis of electronic cigarette portrayal in newspapers. *Tobacco Regulatory Science*, 1(1), 94–102.
Yu, V., Rahimy, M., Korrapati, A., Xuan, Y., Zou, A. E., Krishnan, A. R., ... & Brumund, K. T. (2016). Electronic cigarettes induce DNA strand breaks and cell death independently of nicotine in cell lines. *Oral Oncology*, 52, 58–65.
Zadeh, L. A. (1965). Fuzzy sets. *Information and Control*, 8(3), 338–353.
Zlatev, J., & Blomberg, J. (2015). Language may indeed influence thought. *Frontiers in Psychology*, 6, 1631.
Zlatev, J., Smith, V., van de Weijer, J., & Skydsgaard, K. (2010). Noun-noun compounds for fictive food products: Experimenting in the borderzone of semantics and pragmatics. *Journal of Pragmatics*, 42(10), 2799–2813.

Index

Note: **Bold** page numbers refer to tables; *italic* page numbers refer to figures and page numbers followed by "n" denote footnotes.

ad-hoc categories 18–19; human categorization 21–25, *20*; human concepts, anatomy of 19–21
ad-hoc concepts 36
ad-hoc inference-making 73
African American 58
agenda setting 3, 78
AIDS 11
Alzheimer's disease 23
Apple 13, 44, 46, *46*
a priori 17
arbitrary lexical expression-units 29
Ariel, M. 34

balle (versus ball) 15–16
ballon (versus ball) 15–16
Baldinger, K. 13
Barsalou, L. W. 21
Bentsen, S. E. 13
betalingsring 32, 38, 68
Billings, V. D. 54n5
Bing 38–39
black American 58
Blonsky, M. 11
bottom-up extraction 24
brand images 42, 44, 53
branding 3, 39, 60
brand names 13, 17, 27, 29–30, 36–38, 42, 44–46, 48, 49, 51, 52; high- *vs.* low-budget route framing of 43–53; value of 52
brand owners 52
Brexit 1, 11, 13

bubble 30, 53, 64
bug spray 34–36
built-in motivation 40
built-in semantic potential 78

Cacioppo, J. T. 69
categorization 9, 13, 14, 18, 19, 19n4, 21–25, 44, 63, 78
causal theories of reference 23n6
caviar 45n4
Cavi-Art 45–47, 52
civil-law legal thinking 14
climate change 64
CO_2 emissions 53
cognitive dissonance 53, 65, 76
cognitively oriented language theory 18
cognitive variables 23n6, 24
Collins, L. 27, 28, 32, 43; Juliet metaphor 40
commercial communicative practices 66
commercial food products 47–48
common-law legal thinking 14
communication 2–3, 45; language-based 18; semiotic resources used for 59; strategic 75–76
communicative behaviour 34
communicative ethics, implications for 65–67
communicative fairness 75
communicator 17; choice of words 59; professional 66, 67

compact electronic devices 12
compound-processing literature 36
concept 19–22, 25, 30, 31, 31n1, 32, 33, 35–38, 41, 54, 54n5, 55–57; for ad-hoc categories 22; cognitive function of 18; componential analysis of *20*; identification and delimitation of 21; knowledge and 24
conceptual analysis 39
conceptual blending theory 45n4
conceptual clash 45n4
conceptual components 19–20, 31
conceptual restructuring 45n4
conceptual structure 24, 44; analysis of 56
congestion charge 32
congruent name-context pairings 48
consumer: behaviour 66; with minimal knowledge 72
contested concepts 31, 54
context, role of 33–34n2
contextual framings 48, *49,* 54
control *vs.* credibility and effect 51–53
Covid-19 1, 11
cross-disciplinary dialogue 60
cross-disciplinary positioning 8–10

Danish government 32, 38
decoding processes 47, 51
deep state 37
Deutscher, G. 13
Devitt, M. 23n6
discourse analysis 24, 59–60
division of linguistic labour 23n6, 54–56, 65, 78
Durst-Andersen, P. 13

earned media 44, 45
e-cigarettes 53
ecotax 30
encompassing interactive options 51
English language: "Joyce-principle names" 28; language-typological characteristics of 17; words 5, 15
Entman, R. M. 8, 60–62, 61n2, 64, 65
environmental policies 30
Eskimo languages 14

essential (conceptual) components 19
essentially contested concepts 54
eye-tracking 47, 50–51

fairness: communicative 75; implications for 65–67
fake news 25
falsifiability principle 76
familiar name 34, *35,* 78
foie gras 55, 56
food product 59n1, 73; commercial 47–48
Forceville, C. 73, 74
foreign language 41
framing 60, 67–68; in language and communication research 54; mental shortcuts 69; situational relevance 69–70, *71,* 72–75; stereotype thinking 68–69
Freedom fries (vs. French fries) 37
French words 15–17, *16*

Gallie, W. B. 31, 54
Gamson, W. A. 62
Geeraerts, D. 54n5
Germanic languages 15
Gitlin, S. 39
gold 55, 56
graphic motivation 29
green tax 30
"grey zone" 24–25

hangry 12, 25
Hawaiian pizza 34–36
high-budget route 43, 44, 46; control *vs.* credibility and effect 51–53; framing of brand and product names 43–45; "semiotic cocktails" 45–48, *46, 49,* 50–51
HIV 11
Homo Economicus 66
how-aspect of lexicalization, the 22
human activity 10, 77, 79
human categorization 21–25, *20*
human concepts, anatomy of 19–21
human decision-making 66
human language(s) 77
Humboldt, W. von 13
hygiene 38; sleep 30, 38, 63

identification 19n4, 21
idiosyncrasies 17
image 9, 20n5, 46, 47, 64, 72, 74; brand 42, 44, 53
incongruent name-context pairings 48
in-depth conceptual analysis 39
individual languages 78
individual names 59–60
Indo-European 14
information war 31, 58, 64
Internet 66
interpretation 47–48, 51
issues management 59

jewellery 55
Jones, R. H. 50
Joyce, J. 27; lessons learned from 37–39
the Joyce principle 27, 36, 39
"Joyce-principle names" 28
the Juliet principle 27, 36, 58; manifestations of 42; potential of 38

Keil, F. C. 54n5
knowledge: and concepts 24; consumer with minimal 72; structured conceptual 24

labelling practices 50
Lakoff, G. 54n5
Langacker, R. W. 28
language 13–17, *16*; authority (ethos) of users 56; dominant conception of 54; lexical non-arbitrariness in 9; systematic uses of 2
language-based communication 18, 72, 73, 73n6
language-internal factors 17
language processing 33–34, *35*, 36–37
language-theoretical literature 40n1
language-typological differences 14
law & ethics 67
lexical arbitrariness 28–32
lexical expression(-unit) 5
lexicalization 15, 19n4, 22, 24

lexical (word) level 40n1
lexical non-arbitrariness 29
lexical semantics 68n4
linguistic data 14
linguistic relativism 13–14, 21, 63
linguistic relativity 14
linguistic universalism 13
linguists 28
long-term language-internal influences 17
low-budget route: control *vs.* credibility and effect 51–53; framing of brand and product names 43–45; "semiotic cocktails" 45–48, *46, 49,* 50–51
low-involvement settings 70

macaroons 57
Mandarin Chinese 17
mansplaining 37
marketing 2, 3, 9, 27, 28, 30, 38–39, 41, 44, 45; large-scale campaigns 44
Mautner, G. 3
mead 57
meaning-in-context issue 40n1
mental checklists 18
mental shortcuts 67, 69
Messaris, P. 72, 73, 73n6
metalinguistic reflection 34, *35,* 38
methodology 24, 39, 61
miscommunication 15, 17, 79
misleadingness 50
morphological motivation 29
motivation 32, 37, 38, 40, 45, 58, 63; built-in 40; morphological 29, 64, 69; phonetic 28–29; political 32; semantic 29, 30
multimodal character, of level 3 framings 40–43
multimodal communication 3, 42, 46, 68, 79
multimodal communication research 42, 79
multimodal communicative products 78
multimodal contexts 15–16
multimodal framings 59
multimodality 9, 47

multimodal resources 51
multimodal stimuli 47

names/naming: from ad-hoc categories to first candidates for 18–25; at level 1 revisited, success criteria for 25–26; negotiated 53–57; verbal and visual framing of 51
naming and framing 1–4, 77; aims and scope 4–8; cross-disciplinary positioning 8–10; levels of 5–6, 6, 7; theorizing and empirical evidence 78; understanding full ecosystem of 62–65, *65*
natural kinds 23
nature-given properties 23
negro 58
nerd 5, 12
non-arbitrariness 9, 29
non-arbitrary names 32, 36, 53
non-arbitrary words 41
non-verbal communicative 67, 70
non-verbal communicative resources 78
non-verbal contextual cues 63
non-verbal (visual) framings 62
noun-noun compound name, familiar *vs.* unfamiliar 34, *35*

ordinary language 55, 56
oversimplification 67
owned media 45, 52, 60, 66

packaging design 50, 69, 73
paid media 44, 45, 52
performance-oriented disciplines 43
persuasion 3, 58
Petty, R. E. 69
phonetic motivation 28–29
picture 3, 4, 9, 25, 33, 36, 42, 46, 48, 50, 51, 60, 61, 73, 74, 75
picture-based communication 72, 73n6
Place-Food compounds 48, *49*
politics 9, 60, 77
polysemous words 40n1
Popper, K. 76

positive brand image 53
powernap 63
premenstrual syndrome (PMS) 12
product: development 4; physical origin of 47–48
product-line specific brand names 46
product name 30, 43–53, 60; high- *vs.* low-budget route framing of 43–53
professional communicators 66, 67
professional language, specialized meaning(s) in 55
propaganda
propositional components 20
protected designation of origin (PDO) 52
prototype 68n4
prototypical (conceptual) components 19
public framings 61
Putnam, H. 23n6, 54–57, 54–55n5, 65, 68n4

raspberry 73, 73n6
real-life communicative domain 74n6, 79
real-life food naming, implication for 50
real-life support 11
"really new products" 11
real-time decoding 51, 78
red blood cells 23
relevance processing 70, *71*, 73, 74
relevance theory (RT) 67, 70–73
re-naming 31, 58
resultant communicative products 79
Romance languages 15
Rosch, E. 68n4
Rozenblit, L. 54n5
running communication 6, 25, 43, 78

salient concept 22, 24, 30
seaweed 45n4
semantic motivation 29
"semiotic cocktails" 45–48, *46, 49, 50–51*
semioticians 28
semiotic modalities 43, 61

semiotic resources 59, 72
sensory components 20
sex worker 31, 58
Shakespeare, W. 27
shared media 44–45, 52
situational relevance 69–70, *71*, 72–75
sleep hygiene 30, 38, 63
smartphone 12, 38, 40, 41, 52–53, 56
smoothie 57
social media 44, 66
Sommers-Flanagan, J. 65
Sommers-Flanagan, J. & R. 65
Sperber, D. 70
spin 61
startup 32, 54
Stein, C. 54n5
step-by-step relevance processing 70
stereotype 14, 55, 67, 68–69, 68n4, 76
stereotype thinking 68–69
strategic communications 31, 75–76
strong consumer 72
structural language theory 28
structured conceptual knowledge 24
substitute names 31, 37, 58
surimi shrimps 57
systematic framing 42

Tabansky, L. 76
taxation 30
tentative conceptualizations 63
terminology management 41
Thanksgiving dinner 22

Tracey Communications 11
Tracey, K. 11
Trzakowski, J. 66, 67

Unfair Commercial Practices Directive (UCPD) 66
unfamiliar name 34, *35*, 78
unprotected (generic) product names 52–53

verbal claim 36, 48, 49, 51
verbal communicative resources 67, 70, 78
verbal contextual cues 63
verbal framing of names 51
visual framing of names 51

Walker, F. 39
water hammer 22, 24
weak consumer 72
Webb, L. 54n5
what-aspect of lexicalization, the 22
Whorf, B. L. 13
Wierzbicka, A. 13
Wilson, D. 70
word acquisition 23n6, 36
word formation 29
word of mouth 38, 42
words 5; communicator's choice of 59; importance of choosing and/or creating 3; isolated 73, 73n6; non-arbitrary 41; polysemous 40n1; systematic uses of 2

For Product Safety Concerns and Information please contact our EU representative GPSR@taylorandfrancis.com
Taylor & Francis Verlag GmbH, Kaufingerstraße 24, 80331 München, Germany

www.ingramcontent.com/pod-product-compliance
Lightning Source LLC
Chambersburg PA
CBHW051755230426
43670CB00012B/2302